UFOs OVER GALISTEO

AND OTHER STORIES OF NEW MEXICO'S HISTORY

UFOs OVER GALISTEO

AND OTHER STORIES OF NEW MEXICO'S HISTORY

Robert J. Tórrez

University of New Mexico Press
Albuquerque

10 09 08 07 06 05 04   1 2 3 4 5 6 7

Library of Congress Cataloging-in-Publication Data

Tórrez, Robert J.
UFOs over Galisteo and other stories of New Mexico's history /
Robert J. Tórrez.— 1st ed.
p. cm.
Includes index.
ISBN 0-8263-3435-0 (pbk. : alk. paper)
1. New Mexico—History—Anecdotes.
2. New Mexico—Biography—Anecdotes. I. Title.
F796.6.T67 2004
978.9′04′0922—dc22
2004011808

Design and composition: Maya Allen-Gallegos
Typeset in ACaslon 11/13.5
Display type set in Engravers and Playbill

Table of Contents

Introduction

*"Pasó por aqui el adelantado Don Juan de Oñate del des-
cubrimiento de la mar del Sur a 16 de Abril 1606."*[1]

With these simple words carved into the walls of the great
western New Mexico landmark of El Morro, don Juan de
Oñate, the colonizer and first governor of New Mexico, left
an indelible imprint on the landscape and history of our state.
The nature of his position and actions produced hundreds of
documents that provide us minute detail of what he accomplished. For better or worse, his role in our history is assured.
However, the walls of El Morro also bear hundreds of additional names and images, many that predate the European
presence in the region. Over the centuries, thousands of
hunters, shepherds, merchants, soldiers, and other travelers
stopped to rest and refresh themselves at this magnificent
landmark. Many of these left their own inscriptions alongside
those of don Juan de Oñate. The imprints they carved on these
stone walls are undeniable evidence that they too, passed
through here. Each of those individuals is a part of New
Mexico's storied past. Yet, for most of these, the annals of history are silent.

Gaspar Pérez de Villagrá was a Spanish officer who accompanied Juan de Oñate's colonization expedition to New Mexico

in 1598. In 1610, Villagrá published his epic poem, *Historia de la Nueva México,* one of the earliest histories written about any region within what is now the United States of America. His account provides us an important eyewitness account of the beginnings of New Mexico's written history. In the prologue to his *Historia,* Villagrá anticipated that the accomplishments and contributions of many of our ancestors would be lost and ignored and reminds us why Juan de Oñate's inscription at El Morro has stood out throughout the centuries:

> Through history those men are heroes whose deeds have been given proper recognition by the historian's pen. Others whose lives are unrecorded, so far as posterity is concerned, did nothing, for of these our annals are silent and we know them not.[2]

Considering the controversy that has recently surrounded certain of Juan de Oñate's actions, most notably the sentences he imposed on the people of Acoma in 1599, it may also be said that men whose deeds are recorded can be remembered as less than heroes. However, while the pens, typewriters and word processors of numerous historians have assured Juan de Oñate a significant place in history, our history books are silent about most of the others that accompanied and later followed him to New Mexico.

Villagrá's warning is timeless. In 1940, more than three centuries after the *Historia* was published, educator George I. Sanchez elaborated on Villagrá's warning in the title and subject of his timeless book, *Forgotten People: A Study of New Mexicans:*

> It is easy and pleasant to cloak Spanish colonial endeavor with robes of pomp and splendor. . . . The

blowing of trumpets, the glistening of armor, the trampling of steeds, the manly deeds of swash-buckling adventurers . . . appeal to the imagination and excite the emotions. Colored by sentiment, the pages of history become the springboard for a fanciful imagery which obscures reality and detracts from understanding.[3]

These forgotten people are the focus of this volume. Here are presented, most for the first time, a selection of stories that have remained hidden, if not ignored, among the three and a half centuries of documents that New Mexico maintains in its various archival collections. These documents from New Mexico's Spanish, Mexican, and Territorial period archives serve as silent "voices from the past" that tell us much more than the political, social and economic accomplishments of those made familiar to us by our history books. These documents tell us of the often stark, yet endlessly fascinating realities of what normal human beings went through to feed and protect their families, keep warm, worship their God, deal with government bureaucracies, and enjoy a few of life's pleasures.

This project had its genesis during my childhood nearly fifty years ago. I was born and raised in Los Ojos, a village located in northern Rio Arriba County. Some readers may recognize Los Ojos by its former name of Park View, but that is another story. I grew up in a world filled with brothers, sisters, uncles, aunts, cousins, and numerous neighbors and playmates. Los Ojos was a wonderful place in which to grow up, a place that holds very many fond memories. Among my most pleasant memories of childhood and growing into young adulthood are those times spent listening to my grandmother, Silveria Tórrez, my parents, and other adults tell of their childhood and life experiences. I like to think these stories sparked my interest in history and helped me develop the concept for "voices from the past." Their stories, along with those of don Samuel and Bernardo Sanchez, my great uncle, Lucas Martínez, don Antonio Madrid, doña Margarita Martínez, as well as the other *viejitos* I have been privileged to know, gave direction and substance to the research and writing I have done on the history of northern New Mexico during the past thirty years. I hope some of their spirit, affection and respect for the past shows through in these stories.

When I began my graduate studies at New Mexico Highlands University in Las Vegas in 1970, I was introduced to the New Mexico State Records Center and Archives in Santa Fe. While researching my Master's thesis on Camp Plummer/Fort Lowell, a minor military post established near Tierra Amarilla in 1866, I found documentary references to some of the people and events I had heard about in the stories I had heard decades earlier. The state archives are a historian's heaven. This marvelous place helped me become fully aware of the vast and largely untapped potential of New Mexico's archival collections. For more than three decades, this documentary treasure trove has been the source of countless stories about people and events that have been largely untold and unappreciated.

In 1987, I was appointed State Historian at the New Mexico State Records Center and Archives in Santa Fe, a position I held until my retirement in December 2000. In 1992, Amy Manning was looking for local columnists to contribute positive community news to *Santa Fe Pride*, her bi-monthly publication. She contacted former State Archives Division Director, J. Richard Salazar to see if he was interested in doing a regular column about New Mexico history. Richard was unable to participate at the time, but he referred Amy to me, and, pardon the pun, the rest is history.

When Amy asked if I was interested, I accepted her offer without hesitation. I knew immediately this was the opportunity I had been looking for to write about the little-known stories from our history that needed to be told. It was also an opportunity to enhance the public's knowledge and appreciation of the extraordinary and often underutilized resource we have in our own archival repositories. "Voices From the Past" was thus born and appeared regularly in *Santa Fe Pride* until February 1996, when the paper ceased publication. Soon thereafter, Girard and Janet Iff, publishers of *Round the Roundhouse,* asked if I would continue the articles for their government employees monthly newspaper. The first "Voices From the Past" column appeared in this new venue in the August 29, 1996 issue and has been a regular feature since. This book consists of a selection from the more than one hundred columns that have been published under that byline since 1992.

Few aspects of my professional life have provided me as much enjoyment as the research and writing of this column. It has been the one place where I regularly exercise my corny belief that the best way to make history interesting to the public is to keep in mind that the operative part of "history" is that part of the word that spells s-t-o-r-y. Luckily for me, New Mexico's, Spanish, Mexican, Territorial and Statehood period archives will continue to provide sources for the countless stories that are yet to be told.

I feel that this personal, cultural, and professional background has enabled me to present a personal, yet objective perspective on New Mexico's history. A perspective that readers may find informative and enjoyable, but more importantly, one that will allow a few heretofore silent voices from the past to find their place in history. I can also hope some of these stories spark the reader's personal search for their own "voices from the past." A search that may enable them to feel they too, are a part of New Mexico's fascinating history.

NOTES

1. Gaspar Pérez de Villagrá, *A History of New Mexico, 1610*, trans. by Gilberto Espínosa (Los Angeles: The Quivira Society, 1933), 291.

2. Villagrá, 35. A more recent publication by Miguel Encinias, Alfred Rodríguez, and Joseph P. Sánchez, trans. and eds. *Historia de la Nueva México, 1610* (Albuquerque: University of New Mexico Press, 1992), presents the epic poem in its original form with accompanying English translation.

3. George I. Sanchez, *Forgotten People, A Study of New Mexicans* (Albuquerque: Calvin Horn, Publisher, 1967), 3.

UFOs OVER GALISTEO

AND OTHER STORIES OF NEW MEXICO'S HISTORY

PART ONE

Glimpses of Daily Life

The following section is composed of stories taken principally from two of New Mexico's most extraordinary documentary collections—the *Spanish Archives of New Mexico,
1621–1821* and the *Mexican Archives of New Mexico, 1821–1846*.
Both of these constitute the pre-United States occupation
record of the Spanish (1598–1821) and Mexican (1821–1846) periods of New Mexico's history. These stories cover a broad variety of events that took place during New Mexico's late Spanish
colonial period through the mid-nineteenth century. They
span social, economic, and political events that range from the
very personal (a failed business venture, a marriage proposal,
and a school progress report) to the very public (a tax revolt at
Taos and a Spanish government project designed to revitalize
the weaving industry in New Mexico).

The Bibliographic Notes at the end of each story identify
the specific documents from which a story is derived. Citations
for documents utilized from our Spanish-period archives consist of the description of the document as found in the *Calendar
of the Microfilm Edition of the Spanish Archives of New Mexico,
1621–1821* (also known as SANM II). This citation is followed
by a number commonly known as the "Twitchell number," and
a reference to a microfilm roll and frame. This information will
allow readers to access the original source of information found
in the respective calendars published by the New Mexico State

Records Center and Archives in Santa Fe. Copies of these microfilm editions of New Mexico's documentary collections are widely available at all our state universities, several local libraries, and various genealogy organizations.

References to documents in the *Calendar of the Mexican Archives of New Mexico, 1821–1846,* will be cited as MANM, and followed by a description of the document as found in the calendar, along with the microfilm roll and frame, as appropriate. These refer to the extraordinary but underutilized records of the twenty-five year period between Mexican independence from Spain in 1821 and the occupation of New Mexico by United States troops in 1846. References to sacramental records of the Archdiocese of Santa Fe are from the microfilm available at various locations statewide.

The Risks of Business

A mong the many interesting aspects of the documents in the Spanish and Mexican Archives of New Mexico are the numerous glimpses they provide into the business dealings of our ancestors. These documents make it clear that many New Mexicans were very active in commerce throughout northern New Spain. Much of this commerce consisted of trade with the provinces of northern Mexico, especially in the bordering regions of Chihuahua, Sonora, and Durango. These commercial enterprises carried great risks, not only from the physical dangers of travel and the potential raids by hostile tribes, but the very real risk of financial losses.

Among the many business ventures described in these documents is one that involved a number of prominent men in New Mexico. In 1818, Lorenzo López, a merchant from Chihuahua, sold nearly ten thousand pesos in goods of unspecified type to Francisco Ortiz, José Francisco Ortiz, and Fernando Delgado. The three partners apparently picked up the goods in Chihuahua and agreed to pay López the following year by delivering the equivalent value in *carneros*, or rams (Spanish policy prohibited the export of ewes). Each ram was valued at seven *reales*, or seven-eighths of a peso. This meant the partners were supposed to deliver more than ten thousand sheep to López at the Hacienda de Encinillas, an important *paraje*, or stop, along the *camino real* in northern Chihuahua.

Sheep have been an important part of New Mexico's economy for four centuries. Adele Collier Collection, Image #32212, New Mexico State Records Center and Archives (NMSRCA).

If they were unable to deliver the specified number of rams, the balance was due in cash.

As is wont to happen in business, something went wrong. The documents do not go into detail about the nature of the problem, but in the summer of 1820, López filed a suit in Santa Fe against the partners. López's suit sought to collect a debt of 9,655 pesos, six and one half *reales*. When interest and costs were added, López's total claim amounted to more than 12,000 pesos.

Delgado and the Ortizes did not contest the suit or deny the debt. The contract made it clear they owed López the money. The issue of the suit was to determine which of the partners had the most liability in the debt and how it was to be paid. In this case, the brunt of the debt fell to Francisco Ortiz, who had committed his personal assets as collateral for payment on any default on the contract. Since he did not have the cash necessary to satisfy the suit, judicial officials proceeded to inventory and appraise his personal property so they could place a lien on his assets, pending the outcome of the suit.

This process makes it possible for us nearly two hundred years later, to learn much about the material culture of these prominent New Mexicans. The documents describe Francisco Ortiz' property in great detail and give us an idea of the assets a *rico*, or rich man of his time, possessed. It is clear Ortiz was a man of considerable means. His assets included five homes, the principal being on the plaza of the capital at Santa Fe. His Santa Fe residence consisted of twenty-two rooms built around a *patio* and included two walled *corrales*. This and an adjoining house of eight rooms and its garden plots were appraised at 4,500 pesos. He also owned a massive grant of land six leagues by five leagues square (more than ten square miles) which had two houses on it as well as another ranch at Abiquiú.

These properties and his personal belongings included several religious images and a setting of four silver plates with eight spoons and forks. Livestock such as cattle, oxen, and pack mules, which were a critical element in the transport of goods, constitute nearly half of the appraised value of 24,627 pesos placed on his estate. Ortiz' principal asset, however, was the 14,032 pesos in debts owed him by forty-nine individuals. The list of those indebted to Ortiz reads like a "who's who" of New Mexico. They include clergy and government officials and range from the very small—four pesos owed by Mariano Larrañaga and Antonio Martín—to the significant, such as the more than eight thousand pesos owed him by Rafael Sarracino and Santiago Rodrigues. The total debts owed to Ortiz exceeded the amount sought by López in the suit.

Unfortunately, the case file of Lorenzo López' suit against these New Mexico businessmen is incomplete. The documents only reflect the legal elements of the inventory, appraisal, and lien placed on the property of Francisco Ortiz. They do not tell us how, or even if, Ortiz was able to satisfy the debt. Clearly, this failed business venture cost him dearly. He may not have lost everything, but he would have had to liquidate a significant portion of his estate to pay the debt. Or he may have had to institute his own legal proceedings against those who owed him so he could pay off his own obligations.

While these documentary voices do not tell us everything we would like to know about the past, they help us understand some elements of nineteenth century New Mexicans' lives. This particular suit tells us of the commercial risks they took and of the significant impact business failures could have on the lives of individuals.

———◆———

Bibliographic Note: The information on this case is taken entirely from "*Lorenzo López vs. Francisco Ortiz, José Francisco Ortiz and Fernando Delgado*, June 19–July 14, 1821" SANM II, #2898 (Microfilm roll 20/frame 233).

An Early Report Card

While we know very little about education in Spanish Colonial New Mexico, it is clear that education was very important during the colonial period in Mexico and other parts of the Spanish Empire. In Mexico, for example, schools were established as early as 1524 to teach Latin, music and academic subjects to native youth. Interestingly, one of these early schools was founded in 1532 in the outskirts of Mexico City in a town named Santa Fe. A university that educated many of New Spain's early leaders in science, law, medicine, and theology, was functioning in Mexico by the middle of the sixteenth century.

Unfortunately, this extraordinary educational tradition did not translate well in colonial New Mexico, where there is little evidence of formal schools during the seventeenth and eighteenth centuries. Whatever education was obtained by the youth of this colony seems to have been through a form of home schooling or in classes conducted at the missions operated by the Franciscan friars. There is some indication the wealthy may have sent their children to be educated in Mexico and Europe.

The earliest evidence of public schools in New Mexico is from the early nineteenth century. During this period, local *ayuntamientos*, or town councils, recruited citizens who could read and write to serve as teachers in locations where the population could support a school. An 1808 document indicates teachers were paid through a fee structure that charged parents two *reales* a month per student. If a family had two children in school, the fee or tuition, was five pesos a year for the first two and one *real* per month for each subsequent child. Attendance was mandated for all boys under twelve years of age, but apparently education for girls was not provided, or at least not required.

Our archives do not show at what point these schools were actually started in New Mexico. However, by 1807, one report shows 460 students in attendance at several schools in El Paso del Norte and its neighboring communities. In 1812, a report of the *presidio* company from Santa Fe indicated that 78 of the soldiers' children attended the *escuela de primeras letras,* or primary school, in the capital city. The report proudly noted that sixty of these children could read and eighteen were beginning to learn to write. That same year, however, the report of Pedro Pino to the Spanish Cortes, or Congress, indicated this system provided a primary education only to the children of those who could afford to contribute toward the teacher's salary.

Significant gains in public education began after Mexico achieved its independence from Spain. It is clear by their writings that many New Mexicans felt education would be important in building a strong country. By 1827, several *ayuntamientos* developed and approved formal regulations designed to manage a system of public schools. The regulations for the schools at Santa Fe and Santa Cruz de La Cañada provide a fascinating look at what education may have been like in early nineteenth century New Mexico.

The "Statutes for the Regulation of the general school of this said Villa of Santa Cruz de la Cañada for the year 1827," are among the most detailed and interesting of these surviving regulations. The regulations elaborate on the general philosophy of education, duties of teachers, discipline of students, school term, and hours. The suggested curriculum is heavily weighted toward the study and learning of *la doctrina*, or prayers and Christian doctrine, as well as attendance at religious services. This seems consistent with a document that has at its heading a line from Psalm III, verse 10, in Latin and Spanish:

> *Initium Sapientia timor Domini.*
> *El principio de la saviduria es el temor de Dios*
> [Fear of the Lord is the beginning of wisdom]

A personal touch is provided by several documents that can easily be characterized as report cards. One such report dated March 12, 1830 is of the monthly examination of the students at the public school in Santa Fe. Marcelino Abreu, their teacher, lists twelve students who demonstrated progress during that period. Some of the terminology used in this report has evaded a useful translation, so it must suffice to list only the names of the students here: Juan and Mateo Ortiz, Pablo Padilla, Pablo Durán, Luciano García, Jesús María Sandoval, Santiago Rodríguez, Jesús María López, Jesús Tapia, Guadalupe Sarracino, Santiago Sánchez and José Ortega. Abreu noted that Sarracino, Sánchez, and Ortega knew nothing about numbers when they entered school, but could now do multiplications and sums. It can only be assumed that the parents of these children were as proud of them as any contemporary parent is of theirs.

<hr/>

Bibliographic Note: Information on the Spanish-period reports on schools are from "June 30, 1807, Census of children attending school, El Paso district." SANM II, #2061 (16/363); "July 1, 1808,

(Maynez) Santa Fe, communications and orders on local affairs to the *alcaldes mayors*," SANM II, #2133 (16/554); "March 1–December 1, 1812, Monthly summaries of condition of the Santa Fe Company with Reports." SANM II, #2442 (17/478). References to the Mexican period activities are from MANM: 1827 Legislative, "January 29–December 17, 1827, Ayuntamiento proceedings and general correspondence," (7/124), and MANM: 1830 Legislative, "January 19–June 29, 1830, Ayuntamiento proceedings, jurisdiction of Santa Fe," (11/175). The report of don Pedro Pino can be found in H. Bailey Carroll and J. Villasana Haggard, *Three New Mexico Chronicles* (Albuquerque: The Quivira Society, 1942). A more recent publication on don Pedro's 1812 report can be found in Adrian Bustamante and Marc Simmons, *The Exposition on the Province of New Mexico, 1812, by Don Pedro Bautista Pino* (Santa Fe, El Rancho de Las Golondrinas and Albuquerque, University of New Mexico Press, 1995).

Arranged Marriages in Nineteenth-Century New Mexico

I n the old days, or as we often say in New Mexico, *mas antes,* social interactions were characterized by many formalities. Some of the most fascinating of these formal social interactions involved marriage.

It has been said that until relatively recent times, marriages in New Mexico were arranged by parents, with the prospective bride and groom having little to say in the matter. There are no statistics to verify whether or not this is true, but there is enough anecdotal evidence to conclude that although *mas antes,* some marriages were arranged, the idealized arranged marriage—in which the couple met for the first time shortly before the wedding—was probably rare. In a close-knit society with a relatively small population, most prospective couples would have had an opportunity to meet, court, and discuss their future well in advance of any "arrangement" being made.

In today's society, the radiant couple shows up at the parents' home, announces their intention, and proceeds with wedding plans. In the old days, when a couple discussed marriage, they proceeded much more subtly and formally. First, the prospective groom would discuss it with his parents. If they approved of the match (and let's face it, most parents probably know of the relationship and expect the announcement), the young man's parents arranged a visit to the woman's home to formally ask for her hand in marriage to their son. Sometimes, the parents delegated this task to *pedir mujer*, or *pedir esposa*, the prospective groom's godparents or other close relative, depending on the social circumstances of the families. Some amusing anecdotes tell how a friend or cousin of the prospective groom, possibly on a dare, mustered the courage or audacity to approach the parents of the intended bride. As the story goes, following a brief silence, the friend is rebuffed by a sarcastic comment from the parents about how they recognized the great responsibility he had assumed, but were saddened to learn in this matter that their daughter's suitor had been recently orphaned. This meant, of course, that what he attempted was better left to the parents.

Formal proposals were often done by letter. Examples of these letters have survived and found their way into the archives. One of these is a simple yet elegant proposal dated January 4, 1876, in which Pascual Martínez of Ranchitos de Taos, on behalf of his son Agapito, asks for the hand of María Virginia Gonzales. The letter has been translated from the original Spanish:

> My Dear Sirs, with my deepest appreciation and affection.
>
> It is with great satisfaction that I place this before you, to let you know that my son, Agapito Martínez, your servant, has informed me that he finds himself attracted to your most honorable young daughter, Miss María Virginia Gonzales, with the intent to become engaged and enter the blessed sacrament of matrimony with her; and I, full of joy for his good choice, bring this to your attention so that you may be aware of our intentions; and so I place it in the hands of God with the hope of

obtaining the objective we seek, and you may respond at your convenience, and whether in the affirmative or contrary, I will always remain yours.

No record exists to tell us whether this letter was delivered in person or by mail, nor of a formal response. But since the letter politely leaves open the possibility of a rejection, it follows that in some cases, the girl's family may have had *calabasas* delivered to the suitor's parents or may have invited them to a meal at which *calabasas* were served. And we all know what that meant.

Happily, however, we know that in this case, Pascual's proposal was accepted. The marriage records for Our Lady of Guadalupe church in Taos show Agapito and María Virginia were joined in Holy Matrimony on January 29, 1876, following an engagement of less than four weeks. Four years later, the 1880 census shows the couple and their young family at home in the neighboring community of Cordovas.

The importance of these formalities is demonstrated by the fact that Agapito Martínez, the groom, was at least twenty-five years old, a widower, and may have been raising a young daughter at the time he asked his father to propose marriage to María Virginia. As an independent adult, we can presume Agapito was mature and responsible enough to speak for himself, but he apparently respected the prevailing tradition that required his father make the formal proposal. Such was the manner in which these things were done *mas antes*.

———◆◆———

Bibliographic Note: The marriage proposal can be found in "Marriage proposal of Pascual Martínez, January 4, 1876," Ward Allen Minge-Gonzales Papers, New Mexico State Records Center and Archives, Santa Fe, New Mexico.

Early Weaving in New Mexico

In recent years there has been a resurgence of Hispanic weaving in northern New Mexico. Various cooperative efforts such as Tierra Wools in Los Ojos have established viable enterprises by building on longstanding local weaving traditions. Although the natives of New Mexico have woven cotton and other fibers for many centuries, the weaving of woolen textiles did not begin in this region until sheep were brought to New Mexico nearly four hundred years ago by Spanish explorers and colonists.

Spanish reports of the seventeenth and eighteenth century make it clear weaving was an important part of the economy in New Mexico. Wool blankets, stockings, and cloth were common items exported to Mexico along the *camino real*. There are indications, however, that weaving may have lost some of its local importance during the later 1700s, when the export of sheep and raw wool for processing in Mexico may have been more profitable than the relatively small scale, home-based weaving done in New Mexico. If this was the case, an attempt to revitalize weaving in New Mexico may explain a Spanish government plan to bring instructors from Mexico to teach weaving to the youth of the province in 1805.

The Spanish Archives of New Mexico contain several documents related to an 1805 contract between the Spanish government and Ygnacio Ricardo Bazan and his brother Juan to

Chimayo weavings were prominently displayed during the 1948 Oñate Fiesta parade, Española, New Mexico. Department of Development Collection, Image #2835, NMSRCA.

"teach the art" of weaving to the young people of New Mexico. The document identifies don Ygnacio and his brother as certified weaving instructors (*maestro examinado de tejedores*) who agreed to live in New Mexico for a period of six years or until the students had acquired advanced skills in the craft. The contract goes into great detail on their salary (18 *reales* a day for don Ygnacio, 12 *reales* for his brother, Juan), travel expenses, and other allowances.

An interesting provision of the contract is that the government was to provide the tools and equipment they needed for the enterprise and for the looms that they were to build after arriving in Santa Fe. Sadly, the list of these items, which is supposed to be a separate inventory attached to the contract, is missing. This document would have provided us an extraordinary peek into the materials and terminology used in the early nineteenth-century weaving industry.

The contract also specified that if the brothers left New Mexico before the six years were completed, they would not be paid for their return trip home. However, if they remained the full six years and had taught a sufficient number of students who could be considered experts in the art of weaving, local officials would be allowed to reward the Bazans a bonus befitting their "merits as teachers." Under those conditions, don Ygnacio Ricardo Bazan, a widower, his two sons Francisco Xavier, age 14, and Jose Manuel, age 10, along with his brother Juan, were allowed to proceed to New Mexico. A letter from Governor Real Alencaster indicates the brothers arrived in Santa Fe by November 1805.

There is little else in the archives that provides details of the work the Bazan brothers did in New Mexico except for several expense accounts for 1807 and 1808. Their expense report for 1808, for example, lists a claim by don Ygnacio for 366 days salary totaling 823 pesos, 4 *reales*. Among these expense reports is an auditor's suggestion that samples of student's work accompany Bazan's requests for payment. In 1809, Don Ygnacio responded that despite his limited supply of wool cloth, he would send some samples as soon as possible. It seems that by this time, the Bazan brothers were ready to leave New Mexico and asked the governor to appoint two persons to review and evaluate their work. In August 1809, Governor José Manrrique submitted a report to Mexico and enclosed samples of weaving the students had done without direct supervision of the instructors.

These reports also noted that the project had already cost more than 9,000 pesos, and suggested that parents of the students were satisfied with their progress and seemed capable of managing for themselves. The governor felt the students had learned everything their instructors had to teach, and it was time to allow the Bazans to leave New Mexico in order to avoid further expenses. One of the governor's letters mentions an attached list that contained the names of all the weaving apprentices, but tragically, the list itself is missing. It would have been fascinating to see not only how many students they trained, but whether the names on that list included ancestors of families still associated with weaving in Chimayó and other communities in New Mexico. If these names revealed families that have maintained weaving traditions, it would mean that the weaving project succeeded beyond every expectation of the Spanish government and has returned their investment many times over.

———❖———

Bibliographic Note: The story of the Bazan brothers' work in New Mexico is pieced together from more than a dozen separate documents dated between 1805 and 1814. The principal documents in this story are "September 11, 1805, Weaver's Contract, Mexico," SANM II, #1885 (15/845); "August 31, 1809, [Manrrique], Santa Fe, drafts of three letters on Indian and Administrative affairs and the progress made by weaving instructors," SANM II, #2249 (16/941); and "August 31, 1809, Pedro Ruiz de Larramendi, Santa Fe, re: expenses of the master-weaver and his assistants with appended receipt for wages," SANM II, #2250 (16/948).

The 1829 Census

Numerous censuses were taken during the Spanish colonial and Mexican periods of New Mexico history. Some of these, such as the Spanish censuses of 1750 and 1790 and the 1845 Mexican census are fairly complete and provide names, ages, and occupations of New Mexico's inhabitants. Others provide little more than the number of persons living in a particular settlement or region. The former have proven valuable sources of information for the thousands of individuals who do family research, while others are seldom used because they seem to provide very limited information. When we look at these incomplete census, however, it becomes clear that these too, can provide valuable details about how New Mexicans lived.

One example of an incomplete census is the Mexican census of 1829. The surviving documents provide fragmentary information on only three communities. However, these represent the three principal geographical regions of the territory, San Antonio del Sabinal in the *rio abajo*, the jurisdiction of Cochiti in the middle Rio Grande valley, and Santo Tomás Apostol de Abiquiú in the *rio arriba*. This census was supposed to collect not only population information, but also "the type and number of . . . crops and industry . . ." throughout New Mexico. What happened to the remainder of the census is a mystery, but from these surviving elements we can develop at least a limited view of life in these three regions.

	Solteros		*Casados*		*Viudos*		*Totales*	
	Hombres	*Mugeres*	*Hombres*	*Mugeres*	*Hombres*	*Mugeres*	*Hombres*	*Mugeres*
De 1 a 9 años. - - -	519	618	- - -	- -	- -	- -	519	618
De 10 á 25. - - - -	236	234	179	278	-8	23	419	535
De 25 ast.° - - -	199	196	345	244	-10	19	559	459
De 40 a 50. - - -	79	48	64	67	18	21	157	130
De 50 Arriba	53	47	86	83	14	32	153	162
Total	1082	1043	666	666	50	95	1807	1804

Total en genl. de almas - - - - 3611 #.

Excerpt from the 1829 census for Santo Tomás Apostol de Abiquiú, 1829. MANM, 1829 Miscellaneous, Census.

The report from San Antonio del Sabinal, prepared by José María Lobato, lists only an adult male population of 207, of whom 176 were married, 27 single, and four were widowers. Their livestock consisted of 100 cattle and 309 sheep and goats. Their crops, however, included 1,000 *fanegas* (a colonial measure that consisted of approximately 1.5 bushels) of corn, 300 of wheat, six of beans, 250 of chile, and fifty pesos' worth of onions. They also harvested twelve *fanegas* of cotton and 700 *manojos*, or bundles, of *punche*, a native tobacco.

The report from Cochiti by the *alcalde constitucional* José Miguel Baca includes a table of population which is more detailed than Sabinal's report, and lists 1,476 adults. Baca's report, however, provides no details on agriculture. He summarized crop production for all the listed settlements under his jurisdiction as consisting of an abundance of corn and wheat, which he credited to the availability of water for irrigation. Bajada alone had a limited harvest due to their lack of available water. The adult population listed was as follows:

Pueblo of Cochiti:	182 men, 190 women;
Pueblo of Santo Domingo:	211 men, 216 women;
Peña Blanca:	124 men, 127 women;
Cañada de Cochiti:	125 men, 123 women;
Zile:	48 men, 47 women;
Bajada:	41 men, 42 women.

The report for Abiquiú shows this northern New Mexico community was the most populated of the three. With a total of 3,611 "souls," including children, this report by Miguel Quintana provides the most detail on how the inhabitants made their living. Quintana's report emphasized the relative isolation of this frontier settlement, noting it was located sixteen leagues (a league is approximately 2.6 miles) from the capital at Santa Fe and that the nearest settlements were five or six leagues to the east, along the lower *rio Chama*. He also explained there were no settlements west of Abiquiú except for the *rancherias*, or scattered settlements of the Utes and Navajo.

Quintana noted the temperature in northern New Mexico tended to be very cold and the terrain broken and hilly. However, the agricultural fields that were laid out along the rivers of the region seemed to be quite fertile. He also indicated agriculture was limited by a short summer season and because the ground was covered with snow during most of the winter.

Although the residents of Abiquiú planted wheat, corn, legumes, chile, and onions, Quintana felt most made their living with sheep and wool. While the planting and harvesting of crops took some time and labor every spring and fall, much of the summer and fall was devoted to the processing of wool and weaving a variety of cloth. Every winter, these products and raw wool were taken to Chihuahua and Sonora to trade for mercantile goods. Others left Abiquiú every winter to hunt buffalo in the eastern plains, while some took the opportunity to trade with the various Indian nations along the frontier.

At first glance, this fragmentary census may seem to tell us very little beyond the rough statistics in its population tables. Upon closer review, however, these 1829 reports show that New Mexicans were a hardy and industrious frontier people of whom their descendants can be proud.

—=◆=—

Bibliographic Note: This census is found in MANM: 1829 Miscellaneous, "Nov[ember 1829] Census," (10/389).

Acequia Disputes

In New Mexico, as in any arid climate, access to water is crucial to a farmer's ability to grow crops and support his family. Irrigation was the lifeline of the community and while New Mexico was part of the Spanish empire, and later the Mexican Republic, the law was structured to help ensure that every person who depended on the life-giving water got their fair share of what flowed through the community *acequias* (irrigation ditches). Even in the twenty-first century, much of New Mexico's water law is still based on the ancient system that allocated this precious resource.

It is not surprising that access to water has, and continues to be the cause of legal and physical conflicts between persons who would normally consider themselves good neighbors. The Spanish and Mexican archives contain many examples of litigation involving *acequias* and water. Most were settled amicably, but a few serve as vivid examples of how disputes over water were sometimes real issues of life and death.

In 1796, Governor Fernando Chacón received information that Juan Ygnacio Vigil, a *vecino* (resident) of Las Trampas de Taos was in the parish church at Santa Fe seeking sanctuary from prosecution for the death of Joseph Armijo, also of Trampas. Governor Chacón quickly commissioned Antonio de Arze so he could proceed to Trampas and investigate the

The tranquil setting of acequias was often disturbed by conflicts over the precious water they carried. Virginia Johnson Collection, Image #33233, NMSRCA.

situation. Arze went through the delicate process of removing Vigil from sanctuary, formally arrested him, and secured him in the public jail.

Arze's investigation showed that Vigil had killed Armijo during an argument sparked by an ongoing dispute over irrigation. Armijo had apparently attempted to hit Vigil with a shovel, but missed. Vigil then struck back, severely injuring Armijo, who subsequently died from his wounds. During the proceedings, José Rafael Sarracino, the *defensor,* or defense attorney appointed for Vigil, presented a strong case for self-defense. However, in the manner of how judicial cases were handled in those days, the case was referred to the *Audencia* (higher court) at Guadalajara for review. More than a year passed before an opinion supporting acquittal made its way back to New Mexico. The decision of the higher court noted that Armijo's death, while regrettable, was as a result of Vigil's justifiable effort to defend himself.

A much less tragic, and certainly more colorful story, emerges from the Mexican archives regarding an 1835 dispute at the Plaza de San Antonio, probably in the vicinity of present-day Hernández. That spring, several residents of San Antonio appeared before Juan Manuel Vigil, the *alcalde mayor* of the Chama jurisdiction, and filed a complaint against José Antonio Mese and Luis Gonzales. Seberino Balerio, *mayordomo* of the San Antonio *acequia* had apparently included Gonzales on the list of persons required to contribute to the *fatiga*, or seasonal cleaning of the community ditch. Mese had intervened on behalf of Gonzales, claiming Gonzales worked for him and could not be required to take part in this task. After Mese threatened Balerio and refused him access to the ditch adjacent to his house, Balerio requested help from the community to deal with Mese and Gonzales.

When Balerio returned with help, they found Mese and his wife had armed themselves and threatened to fight anyone who came near. Alarmed at this turn of events, the residents of San Antonio notified Vigil, who as *alcalde mayor* issued a formal order to Mese that he desist from his resistance and present himself before the *alcalde* for a hearing on the issue. Normally, such a formal order would have caught the attention of most law-abiding New Mexicans. Mese, however, continued to resist. He filled his *serape* with stones and threw them at anyone who attempted to approach. Finally, through the intervention of an influential neighbor, José Manuel Salazar, Mese agreed to appear before Vigil. Vigil upbraided Mese for his behavior and Mese seemed repentant, but as soon as he returned home, he used the fact that Vigil had not punished him to brag that he could get away with anything. The *mayordomo* and several residents quickly reported Mese's refusal to cooperate, prompting the *alcalde* to order that Mese be jailed until he agreed to cooperate. After three days in confinement, an apparently repentant Mese agreed to behave and was released. However, he immediately proceeded to confront Balerio and began using water from the *acequia* without authority to do so. His latest actions tested the patience of his neighbors one too many times. Rafael García, apparently fed up with Mese's latest antics struck Mese with his fist, knocking him out so thoroughly that some feared he was dead. After he gained consciousness, Mese appeared unable to speak and communicated only with "feeble signs." Vigil's report, however, notes that Mese recovered fully and may have faked his symptoms. Late that night, after everyone had left Mese's house, he was overheard speaking, in the final words of Vigil's report, "*mas que un perico.*" Thus closed another fascinating look at the occasionally humorous travails of our ancestors.

<hr/>

Bibliographic Note: The principal materials on this story are from "August 1–September 30, 1796, Case against Juan Ygnacio Vigil, Santa Fe," SANM II, #1368 (13/949); and "November 15, 1797, (Chacon), Santa Fe, draft of a letter re: case of Juan Ygnacio Vigil," SANM II, #1401 (14/218). The Mese case is from "January 1– August 2, 1835, Book of Verbal Decisions, Alcalde of Chama," MANM: 1835 Judicial Proceedings, Jurisdiction of Santa Cruz de la Cañada (20/525).

The Taos Tax Revolt of 1816

In March 1816, New Mexico Governor Alberto Maynez received an unusual and troubling report from Taos. The report informed him that more than two hundred citizens of that vicinity had been placed under arrest and were in jail. It appeared Taos was on the verge of a revolt.

Following some preliminary inquiries, Governor Maynez received a petition from Taos signed by "those jailed at Taos." The letter complained of their *alcade mayor's* (Pedro Martín's), administration, and emphatically stated they no longer wanted to recognize don Pedro as their *alcalde*. The petitioners concluded their letter by reiterating their loyalty to the king and asked they be allowed to travel to Santa Fe and speak to the governor. The petition stated:

> We are faithful subjects of the King, and as such we are prepared to respond immediately if the King orders us to pay a fifth of our harvest and property, but if the order is not [from his Majesty], we protest it as ruinous to our families, and beg for a permit to proceed to Santa Fe to present our complaints.

This remarkable document was a result of events placed into motion by a proclamation issued in 1814, in which the

Spanish government imposed a five percent tax on all real property. The governor had distributed the order to the various *alcaldes* throughout New Mexico, instructing them to proceed with collection of the tax. The instructions also cautioned these local officials to be careful that they did not do so in a heavy-handed manner.

Now Taos appeared on the verge of rebellion, and Governor Maynez was faced with a serious situation. He appointed the retired Alférez, Juan de Dios Peña, to proceed to the region and investigate. Peña discovered that in compliance with the governor's orders, Pedro Martín, the *alcalde mayor* of Taos, had held a number of community meetings to read the proclamation that imposed the five percent tax. At each place, there had been murmurs of protest, but there apparently had been no major problems until he read the proclamation at San Geronimo de Taos, where fifty-eight citizens gathered to hear what the *alcalde* had to say.

By now, Martín had apparently had his fill of complaints, and when several individuals voiced their concerns, he lost his temper and contrary to the governor's caution, threatened to arrest anyone else who protested. This only further inflamed the crowd, and in response, Martín arrested and jailed three of the most vociferous protesters. But the crowd did not disperse. Instead, they asserted that they all deserved to be arrested because they all felt the same as those who had been jailed. Martín agreed, arrested the entire group, and marched everyone off to the jail, which soon overflowed into the plaza.

It appears the protest spread quickly. By the time Peña arrived at Taos, he found 280 persons under arrest. On June 26, after collecting hundreds of pages of testimony, Peña submitted his report to Governor Maynez. Although everything seemed relatively quiet at this point, Maynez decided he wanted to speak directly to those involved, and ordered five *apoderados* (representatives) be elected from among those under arrest to come to Santa Fe and speak on behalf of all the Taos residents.

Those elected—Felipe Sandoval, Francisco Sandoval, Bicente Trujillo, Pedro Antonio Martín, and Jose Antonio Archuleta, along with *alcalde mayor* Pedro Martín—proceeded to Santa Fe and presented their case to the governor. Maynez was clearly concerned. The citizens of Taos had gotten themselves into a situation that could be interpreted as treason, charges that carried serious consequences. So he listened carefully to what everyone had to say and after careful consideration, decided it was in the best interests of all involved if charges against the Taos residents were dropped. "[I] pardon equally, the errors committed and insults made to my royal authority," he proclaimed, but warned that all the testimony and proceedings would remain on record and that the people of Taos would be punished severely if they ever again threatened "any such discord."

For their part, the Taoseños acknowledged they had been wrong to defy Martín, who was the governor's legally appointed representative. They confessed to their "thoughtless and involuntary actions," publicly acknowledged the governor's authority as a representative of the king, and agreed the tax had been imposed by legitimate authority.

The big loser in this affair was Pedro Martín. Although he felt he had acted with the best of intentions, he admitted his response to the situation was inappropriate. He assumed responsibility for the subsequent problems and submitted his resignation. Juan de Dios Peña was appointed *alcalde mayor* in his place.

With this settlement, quiet returned to Taos, and everyone resumed their daily activities. The tax revolt was over, and now there were fields to be planted and livestock to be tended. The tax still had to be paid, but the citizens of Taos had made their point. Contrary to what we are often led to believe, New Mexico's citizens did not comply blindly. Through their protest, they forced the replacement of an unpopular public official while maintaining their status as loyal subjects of a distant, but beloved and respected royal authority.

———◦———

Bibliographic Note: This story is taken almost entirely from "March 14–June 27, 1816, *Citizens of Taos vs. the alcalde Pedro Martín*," SANM II, #2655 (18/391).

PART TWO

Indian Relations

This section emphasizes stories taken from documents of the Spanish, Mexican and Territorial periods that relate to New Mexico's native peoples. It is incredible how much time, effort, and resources New Mexicans expended in both fighting and attempting to maintain peaceful relations with the various tribes that surrounded the province. The single most voluminous portion of New Mexico's Spanish and Mexican period archives may consist of reports of raids on frontier communities and documentation of efforts to counter these raids and establish or maintain peaceful relations with the Apache, Navajo, Ute, and other "gentile," or non-Christian tribes. The burial records of the Archdiocese of Santa Fe contain hundreds of entries of deaths attributed to these "enemy tribes." Official reports of *juntas de guerra*, the war councils convened to consider appropriate responses to raids, along with reports of the subsequent retaliatory campaigns and treaty negotiations, tell of this regrettable element of our history. Some of the stories in this section reflect the tumultuous nature of these frontier relationships.

The stories in this section also tell of another important segment of New Mexico's Native American population—the Pueblos. The stories of the Pueblos of Santa Clara and Isleta reflect the industrious nature attributed to these peoples by many observers of the time. The story of the 1910 "revolt" at

Taos, however, suggests how the simple attempt of a pueblo to protect its interests could be interpreted so erroneously.

Some of the stories in this section are taken from Spanish and Mexican period archival collections described earlier. However, three additional sources of information are introduced here. One of the most important of these is the newspapers of the period found in the original and microfilm versions at the New Mexico State Library. The second valuable documentary source is the Territorial Archives of New Mexico (1846–1912), and finally, the federal record group found in the Records of the New Mexico Superintendency of Indian Affairs, 1849–1881.

The Territorial-period archives of New Mexico cited here and in subsequent stories are found in the *Calendar to the Microfilm Edition of the Territorial Archives of New Mexico*, published by the New Mexico State Records Center and Archives. These are cited as TANM, followed by a particular record group and a microfilm roll, as appropriate.

The Navajo Campaigns of 1836–1837

A mong the seemingly never-ending stories found within the Spanish and Mexican Archives of New Mexico are the numerous reports of campaigns against the tribes that raided settlements along New Mexico's vast frontier. Few of these reports are more dramatic than those of the campaigns organized against the Navajo by Governor Albino Pérez in the fall of 1836 and winter of 1837.

On November 1, 1836 Governor Pérez submitted a report to the *Comandante General* in Chihuahua detailing his recently concluded campaign against the Navajo in western New Mexico. Pérez felt that the campaign, which lasted nearly six weeks, had inflicted so many casualties and damage to the various Navajo settlements, or *rancherías*, that they would be unable to muster any effective raiding forces for some time to come.

Pérez was wrong. Despite his enthusiastic prediction, the Navajo apparently resumed raiding almost immediately and by late November, the governor was busy organizing another campaign. He lacked the resources to finance and equip a large force, but hoped to gather at least one thousand militia for the campaign. His plan was to deliver a decisive blow when the Navajo least expected it—in the winter. "I will not accept peace until I have punished them severely," he wrote, "in order to make them understand that while New Mexicans are humble in peace, they can enthusiastically wage war on their enemies."

Cubero was at the western edge of New Mexico's frontier in the 1830s.
Frank C. McNitt Collection, Image #6736, NMSRCA.

Pérez left Santa Fe on December 9, 1836 and marched to
Cubero, where he was joined by the bulk of the forces that had
been ordered to gather there from throughout the territory.
The force of 750 men that answered the muster at Cubero was
smaller than Pérez had hoped, but still significant under the
circumstances. He divided his men into five companies. The
first was placed under command of Julian Tenorio of
Alburquerque; the second under Fernando Aragón of Sandía;
the third under José Martínez of Bernalillo; the fourth under
José Francisco Vigil of San Juan de Los Caballeros, and the
fifth under José Gonzales of Taos.

The expedition left Cubero on December 17 and arrived at
Zuni on the 24th. From Zuni, several operations were directed
into the Navajo country in which several *rancherías* were
destroyed, a number of prisoners taken, and several thousand
livestock captured. Pérez reported that two of his citizen soldiers

were wounded in the various clashes. One of the wounded, José Sebastián, died shortly after.

By January 12, 1837, the expedition was sweeping toward Cañon de Chelly in eastern Arizona, where Pérez felt they could deliver a decisive military blow to the Navajo. That night, however, a severe snowstorm brought the campaign to an abrupt halt. When the snow lifted, freezing temperatures killed a number of livestock. Fearful they would lose all their horses and pack animals, the commanders reluctantly decided to break off the expedition and began the difficult trek back to the warmth and comfort of their homes.

While the details of the military aspects of this campaign are interesting, the most fascinating elements of the expedition are the extraordinary hardships suffered by the troops. Governor Pérez's report makes it clear that much of the campaign was waged in extreme cold and deep snow. Between Cubero and Zuni, horses were utilized to break trail in snow up to their chests so that the pack animals and the infantry could follow. During the action in which José Sebastián was mortally wounded, fifty-four men suffered from varying degrees of frostbite and Juan Lueras lost two fingers of his left hand. In another action, 140 men suffered frostbite of the hands and feet, while one lost an ear and three toes.

The hardships endured by these citizen militia was exceeded only by the suffering of the Navajo. In addition to the Navajo killed and captured, Governor Pérez reported that numerous *rancherías* had been dispersed, depriving their inhabitants of shelter and exposing them to the weather. He felt that more Navajo died as a result of this subsequent exposure than had been casualties during the armed encounters of the campaign itself.

The governor concluded that although the campaign had failed to completely defeat the Navajo and eliminate them as a threat to frontier settlements, their efforts had partially succeeded. He noted that two days after arriving in Santa Fe, four Navajo representatives arrived at the capital seeking peace negotiations. If these succeeded in achieving even a short respite of hostilities, the suffering of both sides during the expeditions of 1836–1837 was not in vain.

⸺◈⸺

Bibliographic Note: Albino Pérez to Comandante General, November 1, 1836, December 8, 1836, and February 16, 1837. May 23, 1836–June 1, 1837 Letterbook, communications sent by Governor and Comandante Militar, New Mexico to Comandante General, Chihuahua. MANM: 1835 Governor's Papers, (19/685).

The 1844 Ute Raid on Santa Fe

The late summer of 1844 was a tense time in northern New Mexico. In August of that year, several Ute *capitancillos*, or chiefs, arrived at Abiquiú with a large number of warriors and their families. The prefect of that region, Colonel Juan Andrés Archuleta, reported that the Utes demanded the return of three Navajo captives they had obtained during an earlier campaign against that tribe. Mexican officials had apparently confiscated the captives from the Utes and now they wanted them back. The Utes also demanded compensation for ten of their warriors who had been killed in that war with the Navajo.

In order to pacify the angry Utes, local officials at Abiquiú agreed to return the captives, and according to Archuleta, they left "in friendly terms." A few hours later, however, they returned to Abiquiú, made their camp nearby and commenced a series of disturbances, setting their horses free to roam in the surrounding cultivated fields, which caused great damage to the ongoing harvest.

The Utes were finally persuaded to go to Santa Fe and present their grievances directly to Governor Mariano Martínez. Forewarned by Archuleta's reports, Governor Martínez made arrangements to receive his impending guests. He ordered some sheep slaughtered for meat, along with tobacco and other gifts to present to the Utes when they arrived at the capital.

Capote Ute braves photographed in "full dress" during the
Wheeler Survey, 1874. Frank C. McNitt Collection,
Image #6020, NMSRCA.

Six Ute chiefs and one hundred eighty warriors arrived at
Santa Fe the afternoon of September 5. According to Governor
Martínez's report, the Utes entered the city mounted on good
horses and well-armed. They also moved about the city in an
aggressive manner that suggested they were prepared for, if not
actually looking for, a fight. At the governor's invitation, they
agreed to dismount, made their camp and ate the food that
had been prepared for them.

The following morning, the Utes continued what the governor described as their "suspicious movements." They defiantly refused the breakfast they were offered and threw the gifts they were given onto the street. Shortly afterward, the six chiefs sent word to the governor that they wanted to speak with him, and he agreed to do so, inviting them to join him in a room inside the Palace of the Governors. Through their interpreter, they informed Governor Martínez that they were dissatisfied with the gifts they had received. Martínez ordered a number of other items brought to them, but the Utes apparently remained unhappy.

Panasiyave, one of their principal chiefs, then began to express his opinion of the gifts in "very indecorous terms." At this point, Governor Martínez seems to have begun to lose his patience, and suggested that the chiefs leave for a while and allow him time to consider their complaints and to send for some of the gifts they had requested. The suggestion apparently infuriated the Utes. Panasiyave stepped in front of Martínez and began to hit or poke him in the chest with his fist. The governor pushed Panasiyave away and warned him to keep his distance. Almost immediately, several Utes drew their knives as Panasiyave brandished a hatchet and lunged at Martínez. As Panasiyave advanced toward him, the governor managed to grab a chair with which he struck his attacker, knocking him to the ground. Two of the governor's orderlies and other officers in attendance held the other five chiefs at bay, while several other warriors poured into the room through a window.

A general melee ensued as other soldiers and several citizens joined the fight. Within moments, eight Utes lay dead. The remainder, realizing their principal leaders had been killed, quickly made their escape from the city. A troop of fifty soldiers equipped with a canon was hastily organized and sent in pursuit of the retreating Utes. A running battle that lasted most of the day commenced, during which five more Indians were killed and three soldiers wounded. The troops, however, were unable to overtake the main body of Utes and most escaped into the surrounding countryside.

Some published accounts of this incident differ somewhat with the official reports found in the Mexican Archives of New Mexico from which this story is taken. One of the most notable differences is the part where Governor Martínez's "valiant wife, Doña Teresita," entered the room just as her husband was being attacked. She apparently happened to have his sword with her and handed it to him, "that he might defend himself." Martínez's official report fails to mention that his wife was present or that he used a sword to defend himself.

Thus ended what the history books often call "The Ute Invasion of Santa Fe." However, as we look into the official records of this incident, one might wonder if instead of an invasion, this may have been an ambush orchestrated by government officials frustrated by seemingly incessant raids by the many hostile tribes that populated the New Mexican frontier.

———◆———

Bibliographic Note: The official reports of this incident are from *La Verdad, Periodico de Nuevo Mejico*, September 12, 1844. MANM: 1844 Miscellaneous, Newspapers (37/537); "September 8, 1844, Governor's Proclamation." 1844: Governor's Papers, (35/1018); and January 3, 1844–October 16, 1845, Letterbook of miscellaneous communications sent by Comandante General. 1844: Governor's Papers, (35/568). Peripheral information on the incident can be found in Robert J. Tórrez, "Celebrations of Mexican Independence and a Fracas at the Palace in 1844," *Compadres* (Newsletter of the Friends of the Palace of the Governors) Vol. 6:3 (November 1997): 5–8.

A Trip to Isleta, 1858

An interesting and valuable source of information about New Mexico during the late nineteenth century is found in the numerous reports and letters from travelers that were printed in the local newspapers of the time. Newcomers to New Mexico were eager for information about the territory and anxiously read these reports, many of which were written in hopes of enticing immigration and capital to the region's sparsely settled areas. In January 1858, Samuel Yost, editor of the *Santa Fe Weekly Gazette* and United States Indian Agent for the Pueblos, traveled from Santa Fe to Isleta and wrote about what was apparently a very pleasant trip during which he enjoyed the legendary hospitality of several prominent New Mexicans.

Yost and John Ward, his interpreter, began the trip one Saturday in early January. Their route would take them south from Santa Fe along the ancient *camino real* to the Pueblo of Isleta. The pair left Santa Fe at noon aboard a wagon pulled by a team of "excellent mules." Their first stop was at the ranch of Nasario Gonzales, situated along the rich bottomlands of the Santa Fe River. Don Nasario was a member of the New Mexico Territorial Legislature and one of Santa Fe County's most prominent citizens. Yost described him as a "liberal gentleman," whose home presented an appearance of "plenty and comfort," and that reflected the hospitality and character of its owner.

Pueblo and mission church of Isleta Pueblo, circa 1890. Department of Development Collection, Image #2809, NMSRCA.

After spending Saturday night at the Gonzales ranch, Yost and Ward continued their trip south on Sunday morning. Their next stop was at Algodones, where they spent the night at a hotel operated by a Mr. Gleason. The following morning, they forded the Rio Grande and proceeded to the Pueblo of San Felipe, where they held a meeting with a number of tribal leaders. After concluding their business at San Felipe, the pair continued south until night overtook them as they approached Bernalillo. There they spent "a pleasant evening" enjoying the hospitality of Don Francisco Perea, another of New Mexico's prominent citizens.

Tuesday morning, they proceeded to Alburquerque (the story included the extra "r" of the original spelling of the name), where they spent most of the day looking for a fresh team of mules. Finally, District Court Judge Kirby Benedict, one of New Mexico's most colorful frontier personalities, agreed to lend them his own team. Later that day, they damaged their wagon while fording the Rio Grande, and repairs delayed them several hours. Unable to reach Isleta before nightfall, they stopped at the home of a man they identified only as "General Gutierrez," who was probably Juan N. Gutierrez of Pajarito. There they received a "cordial welcome" and according to Yost, "passed the evening pleasantly, doing justice to the sumptuous repast spread before us at night and morning."

After breakfast, Yost and Ward finally arrived at Isleta, where they met with tribal leaders. Yost does not say much about the meeting itself, but did record his impressions of the people of Isleta and the hospitality they extended to him and Mr. Ward. Yost was most impressed with the cleanliness and neatness of the men who attended their meeting. He also emphasized that although only nine or ten of the 750 residents of the Pueblo could read and write, they all spoke Spanish. The Pueblo itself, he wrote,

> is situated on the Rio Grande on an elevated spot, and is the wealthiest, one of the most moral and industrious Pueblos in the Territory. Besides their Pueblo grants, they own large tracts of the finest lands in the Rio Grande Valley, which they or their forefathers purchased. They have many sheep, cattle, mules, and cultivate the grape and manu-facture . . . wine to a considerable extent.

Agent Yost later visited the home of Ambrosio Abeyta. Yost described don Ambrosio as one of the richest men in the area, with an estimated worth of more than $30,000, a con-siderable sum during that period of our history. Yost praised his host as a "very polite old gentleman" who was quite gener-ous to his guests. Don Ambrosio's hospitality included a lib-eral sample of the wine produced from his own vineyard, which

Yost judged to be "far superior to any we ever tasted in the United States." Yost noted Abeyta had several sons, but the traveling editor was clearly most impressed by the dinner prepared by one of don Ambrosio's daughters, who he described as "a beautiful Indian girl about sixteen years of age."

After partaking of Isleta's hospitality, Yost and Ward began their return trip north. They stopped at Alburquerque, where they spent "a very pleasant and jolly" evening socializing and playing billiards with Judge Benedict and other acquaintances at the Bransford Hotel. Yost does not say much about their return trip to Santa Fe, except to note that on the final evening of the trip, they approached the capital city in the midst of a magnificent sunset. The inspired conclusion to his report describes a scene many of us have witnessed and enjoyed, and which we all welcome at the end of a hard journey:

> The sky at its western verge, seems a lake of fire, and the lowering clouds so many burning curtains . . . from which shoot up lurid flames, until upon the vault of midheavens is reflected in brilliant colors, the grandeur and splendor of the retiring sun . . . throwing gently a beautiful curtain over the place where reposes the God of Day.

Bibliographic Note: This is taken entirely from the article "Trip to the Rio Abajo," *Santa Fe Weekly Gazette*, January 30, 1858.

The Taos "Revolt" of 1910

The people of *el norte*, as we often refer to northern New Mexico, have long been an independent, defiant group. On several occasions, these *norteños* have been at the forefront in resisting real or perceived oppression. The 1837 revolt against the administration of Mexican Governor Albino Pérez and the insurrection against the American occupation in 1847 are but two examples of *norteño* uprisings. Of all the so-called northern rebellions, however, the strangest was a series of outlandish blunders that took place in May of 1910. Had not the events described here held potentially serious consequences, this comedy of errors that has become known as "The Taos Revolt of 1910," may have in fact been considered funny.

This odd and little-known incident of northern New Mexico history began to unfold the morning of May 13, 1910, when Governor William J. Mills received an urgent telegram from Taos County Sheriff Elizardo Quintana. The telegram noted that some fifty Taos Pueblo Indians had raided nearby settlers' homes, torn down fences, driven off stock, and threatened women and children. Quintana felt the situation was too serious for him to handle by himself and urged Governor Mills to send troops to assist him in suppressing the troubles. The alarming state of affairs was confirmed by a postscript from District Court Judge John R. McFie, who noted his belief that "military action" was necessary to prevent loss of life.

Sensational headlines in Santa Fe and Albuquerque newspapers contributed to the hysterical reaction to events at Taos Pueblo.
Author's collection.

Later that afternoon, Sheriff Quintana sent another desperate telegram to Governor Mills that reiterated his need for troops to suppress the "disorder." By four o'clock that afternoon, Governor Mills was convinced that he could no longer delay action, and ordered Adjutant General A. S. Brooks to activate whatever National Guard troops were in Santa Fe to proceed immediately to Taos. Once there, Brooks was to assist the sheriff in order to "preserve order and to prevent any breach of the peace." That same evening, under the sensational headline *PUEBLO INDIANS ON RAMPAGE*, the *Santa Fe New*

Mexican reported a "lot of intoxicated Indians" from the Pueblo of Taos had raided homes and ranches north of the Pueblo, cut fences and attacked women and children. The situation indeed seemed serious.

Shortly after midnight on June 14, General Brooks and a contingent of five officers and fifty National Guard troops boarded a special train at Santa Fe. At 4:30 that morning, they arrived at Barranca, north of Española, where they disembarked to prepare for the thirty-mile march to Taos. In the meantime, Brooks sent a rider to Taos to obtain an update on the situation.

While waiting for the rider to return, General Brooks and his troops began their march to Taos. About five miles from Barranca, they were met by a messenger who brought a surprising letter from Sheriff Quintana. The latter reported that after his initial telegram to Governor Mills, he had received more information that led him to conclude the situation was "very much exaggerated," and there was no need for troops. General Brooks proceeded to Taos without the troops and met with Donaciano Cordova, the Taos Pueblo War Captain. Cordova was shocked when he heard that troops had been sent to Taos and expressed his disgust that "this trivial matter should have been so exaggerated" in the telegrams sent to Santa Fe and the subsequent newspaper reports.

In the meantime, similar information from Quintana and other Taos area residents reached Governor Mills, prompting him to recall Brooks and the troops. After marching back to Barranca and spending a night there, the troops boarded the Denver and Rio Grande and returned to Santa Fe the next day. The "Taos Revolt of 1910," an event that never actually happened except on paper, was over.

Subsequent reports show the decision to send troops to Taos was prompted by a group of men from the Pueblo of Taos when they tore down a fence that obstructed a road they had used for many years. Earlier, several families had filed homestead claims adjacent to, or on property claimed by the Pueblo, and had fenced off the land. On advice from their attorney, men from the Pueblo tore down a fence that had been built across the road by one of these "homesteaders." They then went to a nearby home to advise the owner of what they had done. However, the owner's wife and children were alone, and the sight of Indians at her doorstep apparently sent the lady of the house into hysteria. When the owner returned, his wife reported a vastly exaggerated account of the Indians' visit and by the time the incident was reported to Sheriff Quintana, the story had been blown completely out of proportion. By then, houses had allegedly been burned and lives threatened.

Sheriff Quintana and Judge McFie apparently telegraphed Governor Mills without taking the time to confirm what had actually happened. It was several days before the national media got the story right. Some New Mexicans reported that they had received telegrams from concerned relatives in other parts of the country, concerned that they might not have escaped the ravages of the reported "revolt." A revolt that in fact, occurred only in the outlandish reaction to a minor incident.

———————

Bibliographic Note: Principal information on this incident is from TANM: Records of the Territorial Governors: William J. Mills Papers, 1910–1912, "Special Issues, Activation of the National Guard to Taos Region, 1910," as well as Governor Mills' "Letters Received" and "Letters Sent" for the period. The *Taos Valley News*, May 14, 1910, *Santa Fe New Mexican*, May 14–17, 1910, and *Albuquerque Morning Journal*, May 14–17, 1910, carried reports as events unfolded.

Rescues from Captivity

Most of the letters and documents found in the Spanish and Mexican Archives of New Mexico are related to official government or military matters. Occasionally, however, one finds letters of a personal nature that provide an intimate peek into certain aspects of New Mexico society.

Indian raids were probably the most terrifying part of daily life in New Mexico for much of the Spanish and Mexican periods. Frontier communities not only lost livestock, crops and other property during these raids but individuals often faced death or capture. The kidnapping of women and children during Indian raids and the subsequent retaliation on Indian settlements by the Hispanos of New Spain was so widespread that *rescate,* a form of the Spanish word for ransom, became the official term used by the government to describe the trade fairs at which many these *cautivos* (captives) were subsequently rescued through ransom or purchase.

Poignant stories about rescues and ransom occasionally emerge from the vast documentation in the archives. Such was the case of Paulino Mena, a young boy captured in 1835 by the Comanche when they raided the fields near the town of Coyamo in Chihuahua. Imagine the surprise and relief of his distraught parents when, five years later, they received a letter from New Mexico that informed them Paulino had been rescued. In a letter dated June 8, 1840, Manuel Ramírez, a soldier in the presidial company at Santa Fe (who was apparently the boy's cousin), informed Paulino's parents that he had just confirmed that a boy recently ransomed from the Comanche by José María Sisneros of Casa Colorada, was in fact their long-lost son. Ramírez assured Paulino's mother that her son was safe and that they could come to pick him up at any time. He apologized for not going to Casa Colorada himself to collect the boy, but his duties as a soldier prevented him from making the trip.

We do not know for certain how long the letter took to reach Timoteo Mena, Paulino's father. However, by the first of August, Mena had petitioned the government in Chihuahua for assistance to bring his son home. "How can I express the emotions that overtook my heart when I was informed [that he was captured by the Comanche]," he wrote, noting the efforts he had made to find his son. He expressed great satisfaction that he had at long last been informed that Paulino was safe, although unfortunately, still a long way from home. Mena hoped he could immediately leave for New Mexico to effect the return of his son, but felt that the constant dangers of the ongoing war with hostile tribes made it impractical for him to leave his family at this time. He begged officials in Chihuahua to do what they could to arrange to have Paulino brought from New Mexico by the first available means, promising to pay the cost of such transportation.

Government officials in Chihuahua forwarded Mena's appeal to Governor Manuel Armijo in Santa Fe. Details about how the boy actually got back to Chihuahua are missing, but a letter from Luis Zuloaga on letterhead of the "Gobierno del Departamento de Chihuahua" dated March 11, 1841, officially thanked Governor Armijo for his help and advised that the boy had been turned over to his family on December 1, 1840.

The three letters that refer to the capture, rescue, and subsequent restoration of Paulino Mena to his home after five years of captivity tell us nothing about the ordeal he went through. We can only imagine the circumstances of his captivity and the subsequent rejoicing with which he was welcomed home. The letters also fail to tell us how José María Sisneros managed the rescue and whether Mena reimbursed Sisneros for any expenses. Evidence from other cases, however, suggest Mena would not have been required to do so.

That same year, for example, Governor Manuel Armijo received an appeal from Miguel Leyba of Las Vegas. Leyba informed Armijo that an unnamed individual at Lo de Mora was holding a woman who had been ransomed from the Indians and that the woman was in fact his wife, who had been kidnapped several years earlier. Leyba complained that this unidentified person refused to release his wife until Leyba paid him for his expenses. Armijo's letter ordered local officials to verify whether or not the woman was Leyba's wife. If she was, the woman was to be released immediately without Leyba having to pay anything. The demand for payment, Armijo wrote, was "neither just nor permitted by law." Anyone who effected such a rescue could expect remuneration for expenses only if such payment was done voluntarily. Refusing to return the woman to her husband, he explained, was the same as keeping her in the captivity from which she had been released.

These are only two examples of rescues from captivity. Anecdotal material suggests that many New Mexico families can trace their ancestry to individuals such as Paulino Mena or Miguel Leyba's wife—individuals who survived capture and resumed their lives among the families from which they had been violently torn.

Bibliographic Note: The rescue of Paulino Mena is found in Manuel Ramírez to Timoteo Mena, June 8, 1840, February 21–December 18, 1840, "Miscellaneous communications." MANM: 1840 Communications of Local Officials, (28/22); Governor of Dept. of Chihuahua to Governor of New Mexico, March 11, 1841. February 2–December 21, 1841, "Miscellaneous communications received from within Mexico." 1841: Governor's Papers (28/1093). The correspondence regarding Miguel Leyba is from Manuel Armijo to Miguel Leyba, December 16, 1840. August 25, 1840–January 12, 1842, Letterbook of communications sent to authorities within New Mexico. MANM: 1840 Governor's Papers (27/1159).

Report from Santa Clara, 1840

On March 14, 1840, Juan Cristobal García, interim justice of the peace for the jurisdiction of the Pueblo of Santa Clara, submitted a most fascinating report to Governor Manuel Armijo. The document is less than four pages long, but is one of the most complete extant descriptions of the mineral, agricultural, and water resources of the Rio Arriba during this period. The document was apparently prepared in response to a general call for such information from throughout New Mexico.

Beginning with Santa Clara and working his way north, García identified the settlements in his *partido*, or jurisdiction, as Mi Señora de Guadalupe, San Pedro, San Juan, Santa Rosalía, San Antonio, San José, a second San Pedro, San Francisco, La Pura y Limpia Concepción, and finally, to the west, the settlement of La Divina Pastura. Of these, Santa Clara and San Pedro are the only remaining recognizable names that have survived to this day.

García opened his report by noting it was prepared from his own limited knowledge of the subjects and information obtained from a number of inhabitants more familiar than he with the resources of the district. In the short opening section on mineral resources, García noted that his informants had no knowledge of silver, gold, copper, lead, steel, coal, or other precious metals or minerals in the region. In the following section on agriculture, however, he detailed the various crops

A bountiful harvest at Santa Clara Pueblo, early twentieth century.
Virginia Johnson Collection, Image #33250, NMSRCA.

grown in the valley, when they were planted, harvested, and
what their market value was.

Wheat, for example, was planted in March, harvested in
August and was valued at two pesos per *fanega*. Barley was
planted in March, harvested in July, and valued at between
twelve *reales* (a peso and a half) and two pesos per *fanega*. Corn
was planted in April, harvested in October and valued at two
pesos per *fanega*. Finally, pinto and garbanzo beans were
planted in March, harvested in September and valued at three
to four pesos per *fanega*. Wheat and corn were the most abundant and important of these crops.

Other crops included chile, horse beans (*abas*), peas, lentils,
garlic, and *punche*, the native tobacco. Onions were valued at

one peso per hundred, garlic at 120 per peso. Melons and watermelon sold eight for two *reales*. Orchards produced apricots, peaches, apples, and plums. The apricots and peaches were valued at twelve *reales* per *fanega*, but the value of the apples and plums was not given.

The report also described a division of labor between men and women. Men did the planting, dug ditches, irrigated the fields, and harvested the crops. Following the harvest, men worked with wool, presumably in weaving, but García is not specific about this. Women devoted their time to grinding corn and wheat, while others wove, spun wool, and made stockings.

The principal sources of irrigation were the Rio del Norte (Rio Grande) and the Rio Chama, both of which flowed rapidly and provided abundant water, as they generally still do today. These rivers flowed freely, reaching a width of five hundred *varas* (a *vara* is approximately thirty-three inches) during the spring run-off but dropped to little more than one hundred *varas* at their low points, at which they ran less than two feet deep. Water diverted from these rivers into *acequias* was also used to power *molinos*, or grist mills. García also noted that while these rivers might be considered navigable, navigation consisted of crossing from one shore to the other in canoes. These canoes were carved from pine trees and were five to six *varas* long and one and a half wide.

The hills and mountains that flanked the Rio Grande valley provided abundant pasture and the surrounding mesas and broken terrain were covered with piñon and cedar (juniper) trees. Three crystal-clear springs that flowed from the mountains west of Santa Clara fed the Santa Clara River. The water not utilized for irrigation by the Pueblo of Santa Clara flowed back into the Rio del Norte. These mountains were also the source of water that flowed occasionally through the arroyo known as the Rio del Oso. The flow of this Rio del Oso disappeared into the sandy bottom of the arroyo.

The exact purpose of García's report is not clear, but may have been part of the information gathered for a map of the Rio Arriba that Governor Manuel Armijo reportedly submitted to the federal government in Mexico in 1841. Tragically, the map Armijo referred to has been lost, as have been the other reports on which the map was based. The map and these reports would have provided us an extraordinary look at northern New Mexico's resources for this period of our history. For now, we must be thankful that at least Juan Cristobal García's report survived to enhance our knowledge about a small part of the Rio Grande valley in the vicinity of what is now Española.

Bibliographic Note: Report of Juan Cristobal García, March 14, 1840. February 21–December 18, 1840, "Miscellaneous communications." MANM: 1840 Communications of Local Officials (28/13).

A Ute Chief

The Utes, or Yutas, as they are referred to in Spanish- and Mexican-period documents, played an important part in the history of New Mexico. They consist of at least seven distinct clans or bands that ranged throughout much of northern New Mexico and southern Colorado. Of these, the three bands classified as Southern Utes—the Mouache, Weeminuche and Capote—show up most frequently in documents of the Spanish, Mexican, and American governments. These reports mention many individual Utes, but few show up in the documentation as often as the nineteenth-century Capote chief known as Sobita (there are several variations of the spelling of his name).

Sobita attained the rank of chief sometime after 1854, when the Capote head chief is identified as A-oh-ka-sach. In 1858, Sobita is mentioned prominently in the correspondence of Albert H. Pfeiffer, who indicated Sobita and his band were very active in Pfeiffer's campaigns against the Navajo. In mid-September 1860, Pfeiffer, twenty New Mexican militia, and a large band of Ute warriors left Abiquiú in pursuit of some Navajo raiders. When the expedition overtook the Navajo later that month, they killed six Navajos and captured nineteen others in the ensuing battle. They also recovered 5,000 sheep, 500 horses, and two Mexican captives. As soon as the battle ended, most of the Utes immediately abandoned the campaign

GOVERNOR W. F. M. ARNY'S INDIAN EXPEDITION.—[See Page 534.]

W. F. M. Arny with Ute and Jicarilla leaders. Sobita and Tomás Chacón are in the back row, fifth and third from the right. This woodcut appeared in *Harper's Weekly,* 22 August 1868. Courtesy of Harpweek.

and took all the horses. Pfeiffer reported Sobita was the lone Ute who stayed with him and the militia to help escort the remaining stock and Navajo prisoners back to Abiquiú. Pfeiffer indicated Sobita had told him that he would rather die than abandon an old friend. In 1859, Sobita is credited with delivering supplies and mail for Captain J. H. Macomb's expedition to northwest New Mexico. J. S. Newberry, the expedition's geologist, noted in one of his letters that "Everyone says Sobata [sic] is a great Indian."

Sobita's prominence as a Capote chief culminates in 1868, when his name appears as a signatory to the treaty by which the Utes gave up their claim to traditional lands in New Mexico and Colorado and agreed to enter reservations. Later that year, Sobita joined several Ute chiefs to repudiate the treaty, claiming it had not been negotiated by authorized members of their tribe. Sobita's place in history was immortalized that same year when he and several Ute and Jicarilla chiefs were photographed with Special U.S. Indian Agent, W. F. M. Arny. Tomás Chacón, the Ute interpreter and scout who is featured in the "Biography" section of this publication, also appears in this famous photograph. That same year, another report listed Sobita as "head chief" of the 373 men, women, and children that constituted the Capote band at that time.

Sobita continued to show up in various reports during subsequent years. As noted above, the Capote did not accept the 1868 treaty that required them to move to a reservation in Colorado, so Sobita and his band remained in northern New Mexico for several years. By 1872, however, the U.S. government was under extreme public pressure to move the Utes to their reservation in Colorado. That spring, two companies of U.S. cavalry were ordered to Las Nutritas (now Tierra Amarilla), with instructions to meet with the Capote and convince them, by force if necessary, to move to their Colorado reservation.

On May 6, 1872, Sobita met with the commander of the U.S. troops and the Indian Agent from Abiquiú. The conference lasted all day, but Sobita steadfastly refused to comply with any of the government's demands. That evening, Sobita sent word from his camp that they were tired of talking and were prepared to fight. A running gun battle ensued as the U.S. troops attempted in vain to prevent Sobita and his people from escaping across the Chama River into the unsettled vastness of northwest New Mexico.

This was the Capote's last stand in New Mexico. Despite Sobita's efforts, the Southern Utes were soon forced to leave New Mexico and settle in their reservation at what is now

Ignacio, Colorado. The existing evidence seems to show that Sobita was not an ardent enemy of the "white man." Under his leadership, the Capote attempted to accommodate the newcomers and fought them only when the expanding frontier forced him into a desperate last-ditch effort to do what he felt was best for his people. It is unfortunate that Sobita did not leave documents that tell us more about himself or his thoughts. However, his presence in the correspondence of so many others clearly shows the significant role this Ute chief played in the shaping of New Mexico's history.

<hr />

Bibliographic Note: Sobita's story is pieced together from literally dozens of sources within the Records of the New Mexico Superintendency of Indian Affairs, National Archives Microcopy T-21. Supplementary reading on the events mentioned can be found in Robert J. Tórrez, "Indian Agents Faced Unsettled Times, Violence in Rio Arriba," ¡Salsa! (June 1991, July 1991), 3, 6–8; and Robert J. Tórrez, "The Southern Utes' Last Stand in New Mexico," Old West Vol. 33:2 (Winter 1996), 16–21. The illustration of "Governor W. F. M. Arny's Indian Expedition" is from Harper's Weekly, August 22, 1868, courtesy of HarpWeek, John Alder, Publisher.

PART THREE

Crime and Punishment

New Mexico's Spanish, Mexican, and Territorial period archives are rich with material about crime and punishment. Two of the stories related here are from our Spanish colonial era. It is no accident that they are both about women and their role in crime and punishment. Ongoing research continues to reveal much valuable and fascinating information about this little-known aspect of our colonial experience.

Readers who want to delve more deeply into the subject of crime and punishment in colonial New Mexico should read two valuable University of New Mexico Press publications. Charles R. Cutter, *The Legal Culture of Northern New Spain* (1995), describes the Spanish legal system, while Jill Mocho, *Murder and Justice in Frontier New Mexico* (1997) analyzes the Mexican-period judiciary. Additional information can be found in Robert J. Tórrez, "Crime and Punishment in Colonial New Mexico," *New Mexico Bar Journal* Vol. 7:2 (Summer 2001): 23–27.

The other five stories in this section are taken directly from the thousands of judicial records found in our Territorial-period District Court Records at the New Mexico State Records Center and Archives, many of which remain untapped sources of information. These stories review some of the infamous murder cases of our "wild west" period, including two cases involving women. Valuable sources of information on crime and punishment for the territorial period include the penal papers of the various

Territorial Governors and the Penitentiary of New Mexico Records. Published reference materials include Larry D. Ball, *Desert Lawmen, The High Sheriffs of Arizona and New Mexico 1846–1912* (Albuquerque: University of New Mexico Press, 1992); Robert J. Tórrez, "Myth of the Hanging Tree," *La Cronica de Nuevo México*, Issue no. 44 (January 1997), 2–4; and Tórrez, "Capital Punishment in New Mexico," *La Cronica de Nuevo México*, Issue no. 55 (November 2001), 2–3.

Women and Crime in Colonial New Mexico

I t is noteworthy to observe that our Spanish and Mexican archives make it quite evident that women were involved with crime in colonial New Mexico. They committed crimes, were accessories to crimes, and tragically, even in those "old days," often fell victim to crime. A cursory review of these archives reveals dozens of cases that are clearly spousal or sexual abuse by a male toward a female. Many other case files show a woman charged with a crime or as an accomplice.

There were very few women charged with "felonies" such as robbery. Most cases in which a woman was charged can be described as social crimes, such as adultery (which of course, generally involves a male partner), cohabitation, slander, and some minor assaults. A review of the murder cases for these periods also reveals that nearly a third involved a woman as victim. Several other cases in which a violent death was reported show a woman was peripherally involved, such as the object of a fight between competing lovers or when a jealous husband killed a rival for his wife's affections. There is one tantalizing 1818 document that shows two women and two men were held in jail at Santa Fe pending final determination of their cases. The report indicates both women were being charged, along with the two men, for the murder of their respective husbands! Unfortunately, the full record of these two intriguing murders has not yet surfaced.

In many cases of spousal abuse heard by Spanish and Mexican officials, it is evident that much like what happens today, the wife often dropped the case and agreed to return to her husband in exchange for promises of better treatment. For example, in 1756, a man beat his wife so severely she was administered the last rites of the Church. After she recovered from her injuries, she petitioned the governor to drop the charges against her husband and requested his release from jail. The governor agreed, but only after he formally admonished the husband of the need for harmony between spouses. The husband was also assessed the costs of the case.

The reasons wives chose to forgive an abusive husband were often quite practical. In an extraordinary case from 1744, Juana Martín, the wife of Joseph de Armijo, accused him of carrying on a affair with Getrudes de Segura. When the investigation was concluded, the offending couple was found guilty and Getrudes sentenced to exile at El Paso del Norte for four years. Armijo was allowed to remain in Santa Fe, but was assessed the expenses of Getrudes's trip to El Paso. The formal sentence pointed out Armijo's failure to live up to his responsibilities as a husband and ordered him to live amicably with his wife during Getrudes's period of exile.

Armijo's wife, however, filed an appeal of the sentence and asked the governor to consider mercy for "the other woman." She explained that her charges were, to a degree, prompted by what she called the "jealousies of a woman," and now that her husband was back home, she preferred their limited resources be spent on her own family. At Juana's request, the governor agreed to reduce Getrudes's term of exile and banished her to nearby Santa Cruz de la Cañada instead of El Paso.

Interestingly, not all cases of adultery or alienation of affection involved charges against a husband. In a 1744 case at Jemez, a husband filed a complaint against the man with whom his wife was living openly. The governor ordered the *teniente*, or assistant *alcalde mayor* of Alburquerque, to proceed with an escort of soldiers and two citizens to the house where the offending couple was living. They physically removed the woman from the house, took her back to her husband and admonished her to live peacefully with him as a dutiful wife should.

Many of the cases where women are the perpetrators of violent crime involve a fight between two women who found themselves in a love triangle or when a woman suspected another of using witchcraft or the "diabolical arts" that caused an alienation of affection or some vague illness. Most such witchcraft cases were dismissed as unfounded. Simple disputes were often resolved by mediation, especially when neither of the parties was seriously injured. However, in one notorious 1716 case of "injury with words," Ana María Romero was banished from Santa Fe to Alburquerque when she publicly called a married woman a *puta*, or whore, in the presence of her husband. Romero was, quite literally, given twenty-four hours to leave town.

Our Spanish and Mexican archives contain many more examples of the criminal and social actions that were and continue to be a part of the world in which we live. When we look back on the lives of our ancestors, we must accept and understand that they often lived lives that were much more interesting than we could ever imagine, and that they too, suffered from the same human frailties that plague us today.

———⟡———

Bibliographic Note: This review was extracted from dozens of individual files in the Spanish and Mexican archives. The specific cases cited are from July 23, 1756–August 29, 1756, "Proceedings

against Joseph Antonio Naranjo for mistreatment of wife . . .",
SANM II, #535a (9/8); July 20, 1744–September 26, 1744,
"Complaint of Juana Martín against her husband . . . for adultery," SANM II, #458a (8/279); and January 20, 1716, "Writ of banishment of Ana María Romero," SANM II, #267 (5/448).

A Colonial New Mexico Execution

A mong the folios of ancient documents that constitute our Spanish Archives of New Mexico is the transcript of one of the most fascinating and tragic judicial cases of New Mexico's Spanish colonial period. The case concerns two Cochiti women, María Josefa and her daughter María Francisca, who were found guilty of the premeditated murder of Francisca's husband and hanged in Santa Fe more than two centuries ago.

In late April 1773, Cochiti Pueblo officials reported to *alcalde mayor* Joseph Miguel de la Peña, that two women of the pueblo, a mother and her daughter, had apparently killed Agustín, a native of the Pueblo of Tesuque. De la Peña's investigation determined that on April 16, María Francisca and her mother, María Josefa, had been seen leaving the pueblo accompanied by Agustín, Francisca's husband, but the women later returned alone. When Agustín's body was recovered and returned to the pueblo for burial, the women immediately fell under suspicion.

When questioned, the women openly confessed to the crime. De la Peña carefully asked if they had decided to kill him at the spur of the moment, or if they had planned the murder. This question and their answer were very important. In the Spanish judicial system, premeditated murder was one of the few crimes punishable by death, and since planning implied premeditation, the manner in which they answered could mean the difference between life and death.

Francisca confessed that she had determined to kill her husband some time earlier. Although the records do not make her motives very clear, Francisca was apparently in an unhappy, if not abusive, marriage, and although her mother initially tried to dissuade her from the idea of killing Agustín, it seems they eventually hatched a plan to get rid of him.

On the day of the murder, they convinced Agustín to accompany them into the mountains to help them collect roots that they used to dye cloth. Later that day, Agustín decided to take a nap and while he slept, Francisca quietly slipped a sash around his neck and with each woman holding an end of the sash, pulled in opposite directions until they choked him into unconsciousness. María Josefa then slashed his throat with a knife and stabbed him several times. De la Peña's report included an outline of the murder weapon drawn along the margin.

The confessions set in motion a series of events that took nearly six years to complete. Following their arrests, Governor Pedro Fermín de Mendinueta ordered both women brought to Santa Fe where they could be held more securely while the case was adjudicated. Then followed a long series of legal steps designed to protect the rights of the women and to determine whether or not the murder was in fact premeditated and merited the death penalty. Although the evidence seemed to leave no doubt as to their guilt, a concern for due process resulted in several referrals of the case to Mexico for advice and review by legal experts. In June 1778 a final referral was made by the Viceroy Theodoro de Croix in Mexico City to the *Asesor General* (attorney general) in Chihuahua.

This final review makes it clear that Spanish authorities felt this murder was a "vicious crime" which needed to be punished

The chilling outline of the murder weapon is drawn along the margin of Joseph Miguel de la Peña's report. Spanish Archives of New Mexico (SANM II), #0673.

to the full extent allowed by law—death by hanging. The report also ordered that their bodies were to remain hanging for several days after the execution was carried out. The public display of their bodies was to serve as an example and a warning to "those who did not witness the execution [so they] may see that it was carried out and take the news to their villages so they can spread the word and instill fear among wrongdoers."

Confirmation of María Josefa and María Francisca's sentence reached governor Juan Bautista de Anza in Santa Fe in late January 1779. On January 23, the governor issued the official *auto de sentencia* that was read to the women. To signify their understanding and acceptance of the sentence, the women followed the customary practice of touching the paper on which the sentence was written to their foreheads. Three days later, the women were escorted to a gallows that was probably erected on the plaza, and hanged at noon. That same day, Governor de Anza certified he carried out the executions, and that in accordance with the orders of the Audencia, their bodies had remained hanging for an appropriate amount of time.

What de Anza did not report was that in direct contradiction to orders that the bodies remain hanging for a number of days, he instead allowed them to be taken down that same afternoon for ecclesiastical burial. The records of the Archdiocese of Santa Fe show that María Josefa and María Francisca were buried that same day in the transept of the parish church in Santa Fe. So ended the tragic lives of two women, a mother and daughter who paid the ultimate price for a crime whose motives have been clouded by the passage of more than two centuries.

<hr />

Bibliographic Note: Josefa and Francisca's story is derived principally from April 22, 1773–October 14, 1775, "Proceedings in the case of a Tesuque man murdered by two Cochiti women . . ." SANM II, #673 (10/752), and October 14, 1775–January 26, 1779, "Appeal proceedings in the case of two Cochiti women . . ." SANM II, #690 (10/859).

The Man Who Was Hanged Twice

One of the most interesting cases contained in New Mexico's vast collection of territorial-period criminal court files, is that of Theodore Baker, who was hanged in Las Vegas on May 6, 1887. In and of itself, Baker's execution was fairly typical of the fifty-one legal executions carried out in Territorial New Mexico between 1849 and 1908. What distinguishes Baker's execution is that he had been hanged once before!

This bizarre turn of events began when Theodore Baker, who was down on his luck and drifting aimlessly through northern New Mexico, bumped into Frank Unruh in Springer in the summer of 1885. They had known each other several years earlier in Arizona, and Unruh, a "well-to-do" surveyor, invited his old friend to stay with him and his family at their nearby ranch. Baker quickly accepted the fateful invitation.

Baker remained at the Unruh homestead for several months. He earned his keep by doing ranch chores and kept an eye on things while Unruh was away from home doing his survey work. However, Unruh was frequently absent for extended periods, and Baker seems to have spent much of this time directing "many personal attentions" to Kate Unruh, his host's wife. According to the reports of the time, a "criminal intimacy" soon developed between the two, and the lovers quietly hatched a plan for Mrs. Unruh to divorce her husband and marry Baker.

Frank Unruh evidently became suspicious and confronted the couple on several occasions. Finally, the evening of December 14, 1885, one of these confrontations escalated into a violent struggle between the two men. As the men fought, Baker produced a pistol and shot Unruh at least once. Wounded, Unruh stumbled out the door and collapsed a short distance from the house. Baker followed, and a moment later, several shots shattered the silence of the cold northern New Mexico night.

Following a frenzied discussion, Baker and Kate covered the body with a blanket and rode to a neighbor's house to report the shooting. Along the way, they decided to claim the killing had been in self-defense. However, their story quickly fell apart when a coroner's jury viewed the body the following morning. Baker was arrested and placed in the Colfax County jail in Springer.

The following night, a group of men described as "a mob of outraged citizens," forced their way into the jail, removed Baker from his cell, and dragged him outside. The vigilantes slipped a noose around Baker's neck, hoisted him up a nearby telegraph pole, and quickly disappeared into the dark, apparently confident that justice had been served. However, a few moments later, a sheriff's posse arrived at the scene, cut Baker down, and discovered he was still alive! After he was revived, the stunned prisoner was transferred to the Territorial Penitentiary in Santa Fe for safe keeping. In an interview published in local newspapers a few weeks later, Baker described his brush with death in vivid detail. He also complained of several physical maladies which he attributed to his experience with the Springer lynch mob.

Baker remained in the penitentiary in Santa Fe until May 1886, when his trial was held at the San Miguel County Courthouse in Las Vegas due to a change of venue from

Colfax County. At the trial, Kate Unruh, who had also been indicted in the murder of her husband, turned state's evidence in exchange for the charges against her being dropped. Observers noted that her testimony sealed Baker's fate. When the jury returned a verdict of guilty in the first degree, Judge Elisha V. Long had no choice but to comply with New Mexico territorial law that required a mandatory sentence of death by hanging.

Judge Long's sentence was an eloquent speech in which he reviewed the legal and moral issues he felt had brought Theodore Baker along the "road to perdition." He scolded Baker for betraying his friend in order to "win and debauch his wife, while she was, in the highest sense of manly honor, entrusted to you." After nearly a year of delays during which the Territorial Supreme Court upheld the conviction and sentence, Baker's execution was scheduled for May 6, 1887.

At three o'clock in the afternoon of that day, Baker, accompanied by San Miguel County Sheriff Eugenio Romero, two deputies, and a minister, climbed the steps of the scaffold that had been built for the occasion in the San Miguel County jail yard. In keeping with Judge Long's instructions that the execution not be allowed to become a public spectacle, a wooden enclosure twenty feet high had been built around the gallows to screen it from public view. About sixty officials and dignitaries, including six doctors, several ministers and four newspaper reporters, were authorized to enter the enclosure as witnesses.

After the death warrant was read to the condemned man, he was given the customary opportunity to speak. With his last words, Baker protested his innocence, and insisted Kate Unruh had not only been a willing accomplice, but that she was the one who fired the fatal shots after her husband had stumbled into the yard. It was her treachery, he noted, that convicted him. But his protests were to no avail. A black hood was drawn over his head, and the noose tightened around his neck. At a prearranged signal, the trap door was sprung. By four o'clock, he was declared dead, and cut down. No relatives or friends came forward to claim the body, so Baker was buried in a plain wooden coffin provided by the county. Theodore Baker had not escaped his second brush with the hangman.

———

Bibliographic Note: *Territory vs. Theodore Baker*, San Miguel County Criminal Case #2543 (May 1886), District Court Records, New Mexico State Records Center and Archives (SRCA) and New Mexico Territorial Supreme Court #309 (1887, 4NM309), are the principal sources of information on Baker's case. Numerous issues of the *Las Vegas News* and *The Daily Optic, The Daily New Mexican*, and *The Raton Range* were also utilized. An expanded version of Theodore Baker's story is in Robert J. Tórrez, "The Man Who Was Hanged Twice," *True West* 36:11 (November 1989): 24–27.

A Dubious Distinction

A
mong the many fascinating stories about ordinary people caught up in extraordinary events is that of Paula Angel, a Las Vegas woman who has the dubious distinction of being the only female hanged in Territorial New Mexico. Paula Angel's story is a marvelous mix of historical fact and historical maybe. Her story is at times so bizarre that one could wonder how any of it is true.

The documentary evidence shows that Paula Angel was convicted of first degree murder during the March 1861 term of District Court for San Miguel County. On April 3, 1861, Territorial Governor Abraham Rencher issued the death warrant that set the date of her execution for April 26, 1861. These few factual elements of her case are elaborated by a substantial body of oral history based principally on a story told by the late Luis E. Armijo, a Las Vegas resident and former New Mexico District Court Judge. According to published versions of Judge Armijo's story, the details of Paula Angel's hanging were told to him by his grandmother when he was still a small boy.

The generally accepted story is that Paula was convicted of killing her lover. Following her trial, she was remanded to the county jail where San Miguel County Sheriff Antonio Abad Herrera held her until the date of her scheduled execution. According to Armijo, Sheriff Herrera taunted Paula unmercifully, reminding her each morning that she had one day less to live. When April 26 arrived, a large crowd from throughout the territory congregated in Las Vegas to witness the hanging. Sometime after ten o'clock that morning, Sheriff Herrera placed Paula on a wagon and drove her to the designated place of her execution. The wagon in which she rode also carried the coffin in which she was to be buried.

When Herrera arrived at the place of execution, he halted the wagon under a noose that was dangling from the crossbeam. He placed the noose around her neck and immediately drove the wagon out from under her. As he pulled away, he glanced over his shoulder and was horrified to see that in his haste, he had forgotten to tie Paula's hands. Instead of being hanged, Paula had grabbed the rope and was desperately trying to pull herself up to avoid being strangled. Sheriff Herrera leaped from the wagon and grasped Paula around the waist, trying to pull her downward. The stunned crowd watched this surreal struggle for a moment, then surged forward, pulled Herrera away and cut Paula down. Herrera protested, adamant that justice had not been done, but he was overruled by the crowd, which contended that Paula had been hanged—albeit unsuccessfully.

At this point, José D. Sena, a noted speaker and prominent Santa Fe resident, stepped forward and addressed the crowd. Reading from the warrant of execution issued by Governor Rencher, he emphasized that the document specified the condemned prisoner was to be "hanged by the neck until dead." Paula was clearly not dead, so the requirement of the law had therefore not been met. Paula was once again stood on the back of the wagon, this time with her hands securely tied behind her back. Within a few moments, Paula Angel gained her place in the history books as being the only woman hanged in Territorial New Mexico.

While the details of Paula Angel's execution by hanging on April 26, 1861 are based almost entirely on oral history, Judge

Armijo's story contains a substantial amount of historical fact. There is even a *corrido*, or folk ballad, about Paula's tragic life and death written by her cousin, Juan Angel. As we read the stanzas of the ballad, entitled *La Homicida Pablita*, we can visualize her trial and the heavy burden of the death sentence imposed on her. We shudder as her cell door closes and Paula realizes the full extent of her disgrace and the fate that awaited her. The ballad even describes her final ride on the wagon that carried her to the gallows.

For some historians however, there has always been an element of doubt about this story. Her case file has been missing from the District Court records for a number of years so there is no official record of the charges against her or a transcript of the trial. Even the death warrant issued by Governor Rencher is missing from New Mexico's archives, making it impossible to prove her execution actually took place. However, this lingering doubt was finally put to rest when the original death warrant issued by Rencher on April 3, 1861 was discovered among the New Mexico documents held in the Huntington Library in California. On the back of this document, Sheriff Antonio Abad Herrera, perhaps still a bit shaken by the day's events, certified compliance with the order to hang Paula Angel. His simple statement, "*Retonado y cumplido este mandato, hoy Abril 26 de 1861,*" ("Returned and complied with this order, today, April 26 of 1861") assures that Paula's special place in history, however dubious, can now be considered official.

⇒◆⊂

Bibliographic Note: Early versions of Paula Angel's marvelous story, beginning with William A. Keleher, *Turmoil in New Mexico, 1846–1868* (Santa Fe: The Rydal Press, 1952) credit Judge Luis Armijo with the details of her hanging. Subsequent publications rely heavily on Ernie Thwaites, "Bizarre Frontier Hanging Recalled," *The New Mexican*, April 26, 1961, p. 1. The *corrido* about Paula is transcribed and translated by Julian Josué Vigil, "Paula the Killer," *New Mexico Highlands University Journal* Vol. III: 1 (October 1981): 63–70.

A Poisoning at Hillsboro

One of the most fascinating and tragic incidents of crime and punishment in New Mexico's history involves two teen-aged girls who were sentenced to hang in 1907 for the poisoning death of the husband of one of them. This case began in March of that year, when Dr. Frank Given, a Hillsboro physician, reported to the Sierra County District Attorney that he had suspicions about the manner in which Manuel Madrid had died earlier that day. Dr. Given indicated he could not help but notice some very obvious signs of arsenic poisoning. An investigation quickly implicated Valentina Madrid, the sixteen-year-old widow, and Alma Lyons, her seventeen-year-old childhood friend. Both confessed they had poisoned Madrid but implicated Francisco Baca, an "alleged sweetheart" of the young widow, as the mastermind behind the crime.

The trio was indicted on charges of first degree murder and brought before Judge Frank Parker at the May 1907 term of Sierra County District Court. At that time, Judge Parker separated Francisco Baca's case from the girls' and ordered his trial held over to the next term of court. Elfego Baca, the famous former lawman from Socorro was appointed to prosecute Valentina and Alma's case for the territory.

Reports of the trial show that Manuel Madrid and Valentina had not been married long when Francisco Baca fell

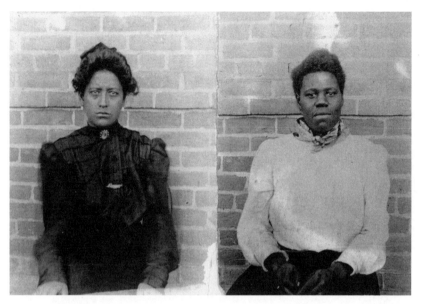

Valentina Madrid (left) and Alma Lyons (right) shortly after their arrest in Hillsboro, 1907. Governor George Curry Penal Papers, NMSRCA.

"desperately in love" with Valentina. Both girls testified Baca wanted to get rid of Madrid so he could marry Valentina and had suggested this could best be accomplished by poisoning. They initially resisted the idea, but Baca allegedly threatened the girls if they did not cooperate. Caught in a quandary, Valentina and Alma decided they had no alternative but to proceed with the plan. With fifty cents Baca gave them, Alma purchased an arsenic rat poison that Valentina proceeded to mix into her husband's coffee every morning. Within a week, Madrid was dead.

Both girls insisted that throughout this time, Baca urged them on and promised to stand by them even at the risk of his own neck. Baca's resolve, however, did not last long. Throughout the girls' trial, he maintained his silence, and when his own trial was held in May 1908, he vehemently denied any involvement with the murder. Baca's 1908 trial ended in a hung jury, and when he was finally retried in 1910, he was acquitted. A newspaper reported that although the jury felt he was an accomplice, they did not feel enough evidence was presented to convict him of first-degree murder.

In the meantime, the girls' own trial concluded the evening of May 9, 1907. It took the jury less than an hour to return a verdict of guilty in the first degree. The following morning, both girls stood before Judge Parker to hear him impose the only sentence allowed by law—Valentina and Alma were to hang together on June 7, 1907.

The alleged love affair between Mrs. Madrid and Baca, the girl's age, the heinous nature of the crime, and the death sentences sparked an outpouring of public comment and sympathy for the girls. Dozens of letters and petitions poured into Acting Governor James W. Raynolds's office in Santa Fe. Most urged him to exercise his privilege of executive clemency and commute their death sentences to life imprisonment. Finally, noting that their execution would eliminate the territory's principal witnesses against Baca, Raynolds issued the commutation on June 4, three days before the scheduled executions. On June 7, 1907, the day they were scheduled to hang, Valentina and Alma were instead transferred to the penitentiary in Santa Fe to begin serving their life terms. When Baca was acquitted, the girls alone had to suffer the penalty imposed by the law for the murder of Manuel Madrid.

Controversy, however, continued to swirl around the girls. In prison, Alma was assigned to do domestic work in Warden John B. McManus's quarters. While there, she developed an intimate relationship with a prison trustee, and soon ended up pregnant. When the situation became public, it took some quick action by prison officials to avoid a major scandal for the administration of Governor William McDonald. Eventually, public indignation died down, and early in 1914 Alma was admitted to St. Vincent's Hospital, where she delivered an apparently healthy boy who was adopted by a local family. Both girls were eventually pardoned by Governor Octaviano Larrazolo in 1920, and Valentina and Alma exited the state penitentiary into a life of anonymity.

———❖———

Bibliographic Note: Most of the Sierra County District Court Records for Valentina and Alma's cases are missing from the State Records Center and Archives. Their story is pieced together from coverage by the *Sierra County Advocate* of May 10 and May 24, 1907, as well as other regional newspapers. Their prison experience is from Penitentiary of New Mexico Records, #2157 (Alma Lyons) and #2158 (Valentina Madrid). A wonderful record of the editorial comment and controversy stirred by their case is found in the Governor George Curry Penal Papers, TANM.

Forgotten Desperados

Followers of the ever-growing and seemingly endless saga of William "Billy the Kid" Bonney, are aware of the New Mexico Territorial District Court term held at Mesilla in March 1881. This was the time and place where he was convicted of first-degree murder and sentenced to hang. It is also well-known that within two weeks of being returned to Lincoln to await the date of his execution, the "Kid" cheated the hangman by killing his jailers and escaping.

In the midst of the attention and publicity given to Billy the Kid's life and death, we have forgotten the many other people affected by that particular court term, which convened on March 28, 1881. Presiding Judge Warren Bristol was confronted with a packed docket. Dozens of criminal cases, including several indictments for larceny, robbery, cattle theft, and one rape, awaited his attention. Judge Bristol also heard many civil cases during the nearly month long term of court. The famous case of *Territory [of New Mexico] vs. William Bonney, alias "Kid," alias William Antrim*, was merely one of seven criminal indictments for murder the court had to deal with. The Kid had to wait his turn as the court made its way through the busy docket.

By the time court adjourned on April 23, one of the seven murder cases had been dropped, and two were continued, or held over for the next term. The remaining four murder trials, including Bonney's, all resulted in convictions. Early in the session, Pedro Rivera was convicted of murder in the fifth degree and sentenced to serve one year in the Doña Ana County jail. The other three convictions, F. C. Clark, Santos Barela, and Bonney were all for murder in the first degree, and all carried the mandatory sentence of death by hanging.

F. C. Clark, an alias for a man who refused to use his real name because he wanted to protect his family, was the first of these three to be sentenced. At five in the afternoon of April 13, 1881, Clark was brought before Judge Bristol. We can imagine the hush that descended over the courtroom as he pronounced the dreaded sentence of death:

> . . . that the said defendant F. C. Clark, be taken into custody by the Sheriff of Dona [sic] Ana County . . . and by him confined in the public prison of said county . . . until on Friday the 13th of May in the year of Our Lord, One Thousand Eight Hundred and Eighty One, . . . between the hours of nine of the clock in the forenoon and three of the clock in the afternoon, he, the said F. C. Clark, be taken from such prison to some suitable and convenient place of execution, within said county . . . and that then and there . . . [he] be hanged by the neck until his body be dead.

Fifteen minutes later, William Bonney stood before Judge Bristol, who pronounced essentially the same death sentence to him. He too was to hang on that ominous date of Friday, May 13, the same day as Clark. The difference was that Bonney was to be returned to Lincoln to await his execution, while Clark remained in jail at Mesilla until the fateful day.

The third person convicted of murder and sentenced to death by hanging was Santos Barela. On April 23, the final day of this famous court session, Barela took his own turn standing before Judge Bristol, and heard the date of his execution set for May 20, 1881, also at Mesilla.

The principal difference in these three cases, as we know, is that William Bonney did not hang as scheduled. On April 28, 1881, he escaped from the Lincoln County jail. Clark and Barela, however, did not escape their dates with the hangman. At one o'clock on the afternoon of Friday, May 13, 1881, F. C. Clark exited the Doña Ana County jail and with his guards, boarded a wagon that carried them to a scaffold that had been constructed on a dry riverbed several hundred yards from the plaza. There, Clark was bid a sad farewell by three Sisters of Charity who had counseled him while in jail. He then climbed the steps to the scaffold's platform, and without ever divulging his true identity, met his sentence with what a newspaper report described as "remarkable nerve."

A week later, Santos Barela stood on the same scaffold, which had been moved from the riverbed to the jail yard, and suffered the fate imposed upon him by Judge Bristol's court. By this time, of course, William Bonney had escaped from Lincoln. However, the "Kid's" freedom was short lived. The night of July 14, 1881, two months and a day after the date he had been scheduled to hang, he too died at the hands of the law. Except that his executioner held a gun, not a rope.

Thus ended the saga of three men who had been thrust together in the same courtroom during the March 1881 term of Doña Ana County District Court. All three were sentenced to die for taking the life of another. One of them, however— the one we have come to know as "Billy the Kid"—gained fame and infamy, while the other two, one of whom's real name we don't know, would be generally forgotten in the chronicles we call history.

———•—•———

Bibliographic Note: The Clark and Barela cases are both found in the District Court Records at the State Records Center and Archives: *Territory vs. F. C. Clark*, Doña Ana County Criminal Case #642 (April 1881), and *Territory vs. Santos Barela*, Doña Ana County Criminal Case #650. Principal newspaper coverage is found in *The Mesilla News*, May 14, 1881, and the *Rio Grande Republican*, May 14 and May 21, 1881.

A New Mexico "Hanging Bee"

New Mexico was going to make its mark on the history of crime and punishment on September 24, 1896. Earlier, the New Mexico Supreme Court handed down opinions on five appeals of District Court cases in which nine men convicted of first-degree murder had been sentenced to death by hanging. The superior court had affirmed all five convictions and as of early September, it appeared all nine men were scheduled to be hanged on the same day—September 24, 1896. The *Silver City Enterprise* reported the story under the headline, "A Hanging Bee," and noted with some apparent pride that the anticipated hanging of nine murderers in one day "beats the record for the west."

The list of men scheduled to hang that day included some of the most notorious cases in the history of New Mexico's "wild west" period. Four of these men, Francisco Gonzales y Borrego, his brother Antonio, and two accomplices, Laurino Alarid and Patricio Valencia, had been convicted of the 1892 murder of former Santa Fe County Sheriff Francisco Chavez.

The other five were convicted in four separate cases scattered through the territory. Perfecto Padilla and Rosario Ring were convicted in the November 1895 term of Rio Arriba County District Court in Tierra Amarilla. Padilla was convicted for killing John Vipond, a prospector, in the fall of 1894.

Perfecto Padilla (left) and Rosario Ring (right), were hanged at Tierra
Amarilla, New Mexico, 24 September 1896.
Courtesy of Aurelia Salazar, author's collection.

Ring, who was described by the newspapers as a hard-core
criminal who had been responsible for several violent felonies,
was to hang for the September 1895 murder of Carlos Ulibarri
during a drunken brawl.

In Albuquerque, Dionicio Sandoval was convicted for the
July 1895 murder of Victoriano Tenorio at a sheep camp near
San Ysidro. The December 1895 session of Bernalillo County
District Court in which Sandoval was convicted was a very
busy one for the presiding judge. One report claims that 110
criminal cases were cleared from the docket, forty-two of them
through convictions by jury trial. Antonio Gonzales and
Eugenio Aragon were the eighth and ninth men scheduled to
hang on September 24, 1896. They were both convicted for the

February 12, 1894 murder and robbery of Charles S. Van Sickle at a ranch near Roswell.

But the record for hangings in one day was not to be. Within a few days of the Supreme Court decisions, Governor William T. Thornton temporarily commuted the sentences of the Borrego brothers and their accomplices. Their execution was postponed until April 2, 1897. The fate of the remaining five men, however, was sealed on September 9, 1896, when Governor Thornton issued warrants for their executions. The anticipated "hanging bee" of September 24, 1896, would now have to content itself with the executions of "only" five persons on that day.

The same day that Governor Thornton issued the death warrants, Eugenio Aragon committed suicide in his cell at Roswell. Aragon "cheated the hangman" by slicing his own throat with the handle of a spoon he had "sharpened on the cell bars." Now, only four of the nine men originally condemned to die on September 24th remained.

Antonio Gonzales was the first to face the hangman that fateful day. He died on the gallows at Roswell as scheduled at 7:00 that morning. Less than an hour later, Dionicio Sandoval was hanged in Albuquerque. The reports of Sandoval's execution present the picture of a man who was prepared to suffer the punishment imposed on him for his crime. He had earlier publicly stated, "I did wrong and I am now ready to pay the penalty." Several thousand spectators witnessed him ascend his scaffold "with a firm and steady step." Perfecto Padilla and Rosario Ring both met their fates later that morning in Tierra Amarilla. Padilla climbed the steps of the scaffold a few minutes after ten. Moments later, Ring followed. His death was the final stitch in the quilt of executions that nearly gave New Mexico the dubious distinction of having carried out the most hangings in one day.

Despite the fact that "only" four men were ultimately hanged on September 24, 1896, many greeted the day as a victory for law and order in New Mexico. The September 25 issue of the *Roswell Record* defiantly stated that those who viewed New Mexico as a place "where law and order are not enforced" needed to pay attention to the events of the previous day. The multiple executions were to be a warning to law-breakers that the lax law enforcement that characterized New Mexico's "wild west" days was coming to an end.

⟫⟪

Bibliographic Note: Details on the Rosario Ring and Perfecto Padilla execution can be found in Robert J. Tórrez, "Murder, Politics, and the Administration of Justice in Frontier New Mexico," *La Cronica de Nuevo México*, Number 32 (December 1991), 2–4. The story behind the hanging of Antonio Gonzales and suicide of Eugenio Aragon are in Elvis Fleming, "First Chaves County Murder Was in 1890s," *Vistas* (*Roswell Daily Record*), November 11 and December 16, 1991 and January 13, 1992. Dionicio Sandoval's case is found in *Territory vs. Dionicio Sandoval*, Bernalillo County District Court Criminal Case #1842 (November 1895), State Records Center and Archives. The subsequent execution of the Borrego brothers and their two accomplices is reported in the *Santa Fe Daily New Mexican*, April 2, 1897.

PART FOUR

Territorial Topics

For all practical purposes, New Mexico became part of the United States on August 18, 1846. That day, the American Army of the West under General Stephen Watts Kearney occupied Santa Fe during the opening stages of the United States-Mexican War of 1846–1848. Following a period of nominal civilian government conducted under the watchful eye of military authorities, New Mexico was officially annexed by the U.S. Congress when the Treaty of Guadalupe Hidalgo was signed on February 2, 1848. Granted Territorial status by the Congress in 1850, New Mexico made several attempts to gain statehood before it finally became the forty-seventh state of the Union in 1912.

The stories in this section take place during the period following the U.S. occupation in 1846 and up to the day New Mexico finally became part of the American Union in 1912. Three of these stories center on events that took place in the oldest and most recognized building in Santa Fe—the Palace of the Governors. The Palace has been the seat of government in New Mexico since the *villa de Santa Fe* was established in 1610. For nearly two-and-a-half centuries, it was office and home to dozens of Spanish and Mexican government officials and continued to serve that purpose under the U.S. government. These stories utilize New Mexico's own territorial-period archives and federal records to tell of the often bizarre events that took place around the ancient *palacio* and the colorful officials that occupied it.

The remaining stories utilize newspapers and business records to describe some of the enterprise and progress that characterized this period of our history. Others will show how the citizens of territorial New Mexico managed to entertain themselves and maybe even found opportunities to tell a few tall stories themselves.

The Governor's Well

ew buildings in the United States can boast the long and colorful history of the Palace of the Governors in Santa Fe. The Palace can trace its beginnings to 1610, when the Spanish government moved its capital from San Gabriel to the newly established *villa de Santa Fe*. During the nearly four centuries that followed, the buildings that constituted the *casas reales*, or Spanish government buildings of which the Palace was a part, have undergone so many changes that we have no real idea what they may have looked like three hundred years ago. The buildings where the Palace now sits were destroyed during the Pueblo Revolt of 1680 and completely rebuilt following Diego de Vargas's *reconquista* of 1693. Several major reconstructions followed during the subsequent three centuries, culminating in the last major renovation in 1913, when the Palace attained its current appearance.

During past centuries, the Palace has served as the seat of government and home for Spanish, Mexican, and American governors as well as the meeting site for the territorial legislature and offices for countless territorial and federal officials. For a few weeks in 1862, even the Confederate flag flew over this venerable old building. If walls could hear and were capable of speaking, what stories these could tell!

Since that is not possible, what we know about the Palace of the Governors has to be extracted from reports and letters of the various governors and other officials who utilized it. One particularly interesting letter was written by Marsh Giddings, who served as New Mexico's territorial governor from 1871 through 1875. Giddings's letter provides a vivid peek at what daily life in Santa Fe may have been like for Giddings and his family. The letter also includes a surprisingly frank expression of how the governor felt about New Mexico and its people.

The letter has its origins in a dispute between Governor Giddings and Eldridge Little, Santa Fe's resident Collector of Internal Revenue for the United States Department of the Treasury. Little worked in the United States Depository, which served as a bank for the deposit and distribution of federal funds in New Mexico. The Depository was located at the southwestern corner of the Palace, and directly adjoined the governor's residence. In late summer, 1873, Little wrote to Washington D.C. and complained to his boss, Treasury Secretary William Richards, that Governor Giddings had refused him access to the well located on the grounds behind the governor's house. Little charged that Giddings had chased his servant, or "watchman," from the grounds with "threatenings and insults." Giddings's subsequent letter, dated August 23, 1873, is in response to a letter he received from the Secretary of Interior concerning Little's complaint.

Governor Giddings explained that the well in question was located in the *placita*, or enclosed courtyard immediately behind the kitchen at the rear of the governor's residence. The governor's kitchen help did their work in this courtyard. It also contained the wood pile, a flower garden, and coop where they raised chickens and turkeys. More importantly, the women and children of the house had to cross the courtyard to get to the "privy." The *placita* and consequently, the well, he complained, were "as much a part of the house as the kitchen." He explained that several weeks earlier, the man Little employed as a watchman had entered this *placita* through a gate in the wall that separated it from the Depository's back yard and had taken water from the well. Giddings suggested that since the well was low and what little water it had was "roily," or very muddy, Little could obtain better water from another nearby source.

However, Little's employee kept coming into the courtyard and helped himself to what little water there was. On several occasions, the gate had been left open, allowing the governor's turkeys and chickens to conveniently escape into Little's yard.

The dispute slowly escalated until in exasperation, Giddings warned the man that he would "break his infernal legs" if that was what it took to keep him out of the yard. Governor Giddings also complained that a number of his tools were missing, prompting him to reveal that what he may have really been complaining about was not water, or even any duplicity on the part of Little, but rather, Giddings's feelings about Mexican character. "There is no trouble about water here," Giddings wrote,

> It is now a mere question whether I shall permit Mr. Little, or what is worse, his Mexican servant . . . to show his disregard for my words and insult me. [M]y Mexican servant . . . can beat his, in stealing on a fair trial [but] he can't do it as long as his man has free access to my wood pile, chickens, and tools, through the gate, and my man has to get over a 14 foot adobe wall. I am confident my man can beat him in a fair trial, because I know that with all my lock keys, bolt bars and drawers many little things get spirited away whatever Mexican we employ without *exception* [emphasis Giddings's].

Governor Giddings indicated he was "mortified beyond measure" that Little's complaint could prompt several of the highest officials in the country to waste their time on a matter "so unworthy of a single moment of their attention." Personally, he noted, the president had appointed him to manage a territory whose 100,000 Mexican subjects made the task "more difficult than the management or executive duties of any three of the other Territories," and he was too busy to devote more time to such "trifling affairs."

The extant correspondence and other records do not show if Giddings and Little ever settled their differences. Giddings's letter, however, may explain why José M. Gallegos, New Mexico's delegate to Congress, had earlier been prompted to comment that Giddings was "an offensive, meddling, disagreeable man to my people."

Giddings's administration was marked by several political controversies and personal tragedies, not the least was the death of his infant grandson at the Palace in February 1875. Giddings himself died at the Palace on June 3, 1875, following a long illness. The newspaper report of his death indicated his family was taking the body "back east" to Michigan for burial. One might wonder if the dirty water in his well may have had something to do with these deaths.

Bibliographic Note: Giddings's letter is found in the Department of Interior Territorial Papers: New Mexico, 1851–1914. National Archives Microfilm, Microcopy 364, Roll 8.

A Fight Over the Territorial Seal

At noon, March 19, 1864, a strange scene was developing at the Palace of the Governors. Santa Fe County Sheriff Juan Moya and a small group of men entered the office of Acting Territorial Secretary Theodore S. Grenier armed with "heavy clubs." Sheriff Moya was there to serve Grenier with a writ of replevin signed by District Court Judge Kirby Benedict that ordered the acting secretary to turn over the "Great Seal of the Territory of New Mexico" to Governor Henry Connelly. The following moments were a confusing blur of activity and shouting, as Sheriff Moya "took hold" of Grenier and demanded the immediate return of the seal. Grenier protested and begged Moya to allow him to consult with the United States District Attorney, whose office was nearby. All the while, Territorial Attorney General Charles P. Cleaver stood at the doorway brandishing a "club cane" in his hand, shouting to Sheriff Moya that he ignore anything Grenier had to say and to carry out the writ immediately. The action subsided when the U.S. District Attorney, whose name is not mentioned, entered the scene and advised Grenier to hand the seal over to Sheriff Moya. Moya's notation on the writ indicates he personally handed the seal to Governor Connelly that same day.

This tense moment in New Mexico's frequently strange history involves several prominent individuals in New Mexico's territorial government. The incident stems from a March 7, 1864

CRESCIT EUNDO

MDCCCL.

New Mexico Territorial Seal, 1866. Author's collection.

note that Governor Connelly sent to Acting Territorial Secretary Grenier. Connelly advised Grenier that he had appointed Demetrio Pérez to the office of Territorial Librarian and asked that Pérez be issued the official commission or appointment to the position. Grenier refused, informing the governor that he could not issue such a document and place the Territorial Seal on it because "there was no vacancy in the office of Librarian." After several days of inaction, an angry governor personally wrote out Pérez's commission, walked into Grenier's office, and demanded the seal. Once again, Grenier refused. On March 19, Governor Connelly, frustrated by Grenier's persistent refusals, went before Chief Justice Kirby Benedict and filed a suit for replevin of the seal. Connelly noted that as governor, he "was entitled to the immediate possession of the great seal" which Grenier "wrongfully detained." Judge Benedict issued the writ that same day to Sheriff Moya, and the scene described earlier then ensued.

At first glance, it seems Governor Connelly overstepped his authority because the territorial secretary was official custodian of the seal. So how was it that Connelly found it necessary to demand it from Grenier? The series of events that led up to this began in September 1862, when Governor Connelly took a leave of absence from the office due to his health and left New Mexico to seek treatment "in the states." As specified by law, Territorial Secretary William F. M. Arny assumed the executive office as acting governor.

Theodore S. Grenier entered the scene when Arny appointed him Territorial Librarian on January 23, 1863. As librarian, Grenier's primary duty was to take care of the Law Library but apparently, Arny utilized Grenier's clerical skills to perform some of the duties of territorial secretary. All was in order until Arny, who was involved in a myriad of territorial affairs, found it necessary to leave Santa Fe on extended journeys. On these occasions, Arny appointed Grenier as "Acting Secretary of the Territory of New Mexico," an action that may have exceeded his authority because this appointment also gave Grenier the responsibility of being acting governor when Arny and Connelly were both absent from the territory!

This arrangement was apparently not a major problem until early February 1864, when Arny took an extended trip to Washington, D.C. Before leaving, he issued one of his "acting secretary" appointments to Grenier. In the meantime, Governor Connelly returned from his own leave of absence and took it upon himself to exercise an executive prerogative by appointing Demetrio Pérez as Territorial Librarian. When Grenier refused to issue Pérez's commission and place the Territorial Seal on it, he appeared to take the "high moral ground" by refusing to obey an order he deemed improper. However, it seems he was simply trying to protect a job to which he had been appointed by Arny the previous year.

When all was said and done, the court compelled Grenier to turn the seal over to Governor Connelly and Pérez was commissioned Territorial Librarian. When Arny returned from Washington, he resumed his duties as secretary and Grenier ended up unemployed. He was also assessed the costs of the replevin suit. A few days later, an editorial in *The New Mexican* commented that everyone would have been saved a lot of trouble if Governor Connelly had simply taken Grenier "by the nape of the neck and toss[ed] him into the middle of the plaza." Maybe so, but then we would have had a whole different slant on the story about "the fight over the territorial seal."

———

Bibliographic Note: Details on the Territorial Seal controversy are found in the Governor's Executive Book #1, Records of the Secretary of the Territory. TANM Roll 21. The *Rio Abajo Weekly Press* of Albuquerque, April 5, 1864 also carries an extensive story on the issue. A history of New Mexico's official seal is in Robert J. Tórrez, "State Seal Receives Eagle-eyed Scrutiny," *New Mexico Magazine* 71:12 (December 1993): 80–87.

Stagecoaches and the Mail
in Early Territorial New Mexico

Among the many fascinating documents at the State Records Center and Archives is a beautiful leather-bound ledger that contains records of T. F. Bowler, an early United States Mail contractor for the route between Santa Fe and El Paso, Texas. The opening entry in the ledger is dated July 10, 1858 and provides details of the first trip taken by the stage along a designated route from Santa Fe through Albuquerque and on to Doña Ana and El Paso. Between that opening day and the closing entry in the ledger dated July 21, 1862, the route varied only slightly, noting stops at Algodones, Bernalillo, La Joya, Lemitar, Socorro, Las Cruces, Mesilla, and various points in between.

The ledger shows Elias Brevoort, an individual who had numerous interests in territorial New Mexico, and a Mr. Godfrey, were the first passengers. Their one-way fare from Santa Fe to El Paso was $30.00, an expensive trip, considering that $30.00 was a typical monthly wage for the average worker of the time. Subsequent trips show many names familiar to students of that period in New Mexico history.

The Bowler stage left Santa Fe on its first trip at 8:00 A.M., July 10, and arrived at El Paso on July 17, seven days later. The ledger shows the coach was pulled by a six mule harness, and conducted, or driven by Joseph W. Corkins and two assistants, Juan de Dios and Jesús, whose last names were not given. They were armed with two Colt revolvers and a carbine. Their cargo also included unspecified "camp utensils," presumably for use when the stage stopped overnight during the week-long trip.

Although these stages carried passengers and packages, all of which are listed in great detail in the ledger, their principal purpose was to deliver the mail along the specified route. An announcement placed in the July 25, 1858 *Santa Fe Weekly Gazette* by mail contractor George H. Giddings noted that his agreement with the postmaster general called for semi-monthly mail service to El Paso. He offered to carry passengers and freight along with the mail, leaving Santa Fe the morning after the mail arrived from Independence, Missouri and arriving at El Paso in eight days. Ledger entries indicate the contractors generally had little trouble meeting that schedule.

By 1862, the contract specifications for the mail route between Santa Fe and Las Cruces reduced the expected length of the trip from seven to five days. Late that year, "Cottril, Viceroy and Company" published an advertisement boasting that their "Fast Stage Line" would make the trip from Santa Fe to Las Cruces "IN THREE DAYS." They planned to leave Santa Fe every Saturday at 8:00 A.M. and arrive in Las Cruces Tuesday morning at 8:00 A.M. The advertisement boasted:

> We are now running our new, comfortable and commodious stage regularly via, Albuquerque, Peralta, Los Lunas, Sabinal, Polvadera, Socorro, Fort Craig, Paraje and Doña Ana. Passengers will find this one of the best and quickest stage lines . . . stocked with fine American horses, and new coaches; accommodating conductors and careful drivers; stopping at the best hotels in the country

for meals; making the trip four days quicker than ever before.

Equal service and speed were promised for the return trip.

We have a brief written account of part of one of these stage trips which provides us an idea of what it was like to travel on an uncomfortable vehicle over rough, if not almost non-existent roads. In a letter published in the December 15, 1863 issue of Albuquerque's *Rio Abajo Weekly Press*, an unidentified gentleman described his journey by stage from Albuquerque to Santa Fe. The writer noted the "cold weather and wretched condition of the roads," especially between Albuquerque and Sandia Pueblo, and credited the driver and passengers for "rendering pleasant what might otherwise have been a disagreeable journey." The stage apparently traveled through the night and stopped at Algodones at two o'clock in the morning for "an excellent supper" at the home of Doña Petra Gurule. Continuing north, they arrived at the *rancho* of don Nicolas Pino, near what is now La Cienega, where they had a "first-rate breakfast." After resting for two hours, they continued on the final leg of the trip to Santa Fe without incident.

Whenever we groan about the one-hour automobile commute between Santa Fe and Albuquerque or the eight hours it takes to drive across the state, we may want to reflect on the time and resources our ancestors invested to make such a trip. Certainly, this may be one aspect of the "good old days" we can do without.

―――――――

Bibliographic Note: This "Way Bill Ledger Book of a U. S. Mail Stage Line," can be found in the Miscellaneous Economic Records: Stagecoaches, New Mexico State Records Center and Archives.

The Telegraph Arrives in New Mexico

Two technological marvels were closely monitored and eagerly anticipated in New Mexico as they advanced westward from the industrial East. Following the Civil War, newspapers in the territory eagerly reported the progress of railroads and the telegraph and speculated on every rumor that hinted of when these harbingers of progress might arrive in the territory. Although the railroad did not arrive in New Mexico until 1879, the other highly anticipated technological wonder of that time, the telegraph, reached the territory more than a decade earlier.

Telegraphic communications between Santa Fe and the "rest of mankind" were established on July 8, 1868. The report of this monumental advance in communication noted that the line had been "so skillfully constructed" that dispatches were sent and received that same evening. According to the *Santa Fe Daily New Mexican,* one of the first messages sent from the city was to President Andrew Johnson:

> We, the citizens of Santa Fe, greet you as president of this Republic on the consumation [sic] of this work, a sure evidence of our determination to keep pace with the spirit and progress of the times.

President Johnson's response, delivered through Territorial Delegate Charles P. Cleaver, was short and simple: "I heartily join my fellow citizens in congratulations." Other messages of congratulations were received, typified by the one from J. K. Graves of Dubuque, Iowa, who noted, "I greet you by electricity. . . . May New Mexico continue to encourage enterprise. . . . Friends in New Mexico, may you ever prosper."

Not surprisingly, this report was accompanied by a story speculating on the "future of Santa Fe" at such time when the railroad arrived in the territory. Ten years before the event actually happened, the prevailing fear was that the rail line would bypass the capital city. Not to worry, noted one newspaper, even if the railroad did not come directly to town, Santa Fe was destined to remain an "important town" not only because of its status as capital, but as a "centre of great trade."

In 1868, however, that concern was still one of speculation, and for now, the telegraph provided ample evidence that progress had not bypassed New Mexico. Within days, columns of national and world news began to appear in local newspapers, along with the notation that these news items had been received by telegraph. Like all progress, however, this latest technological wonder was not without its problems. Less than two weeks after the line was completed, interruptions in service were noted due to stormy weather that caused atmospheric conditions "charged with electricity." In late July, lightning reportedly struck a telegraph pole near the Delgado residence on State Road. The lightning strike caused only minor damage, but an unidentified boy who happened to be walking nearby was knocked to the ground. Fortunately, the boy was not injured.

Business problems were also reported. In early August, the telegraph company issued rules that required all messages be pre-paid. Apparently, there was a mounting problem with the collection of fees by recipients. Published rates show the cost of sending a telegram between Santa Fe and Denver, Colorado was $3.50 for the first ten words, and twenty-three cents for each additional word. Considering that $3.50 was more than the average person earned for a daily wage, this newest technology was clearly expensive.

Arrival of the telegraph at Santa Fe, however, should not overshadow the fact that progress of the line did not pause at the capital city. Construction continued immediately south toward Albuquerque, eventually arriving in Mesilla and other major communities in New Mexico. The quick progress of construction through New Mexico makes one wonder what arrangements were made to acquire right-of-way from the Pueblos and other private land owners on whose property the telegraph line was constructed.

In 1876, less than a decade after its initial construction, the telegraph line between Santa Fe and Albuquerque was described as "a fine piece of work, symmetrical and durable." The poles were noted to have been of a uniform size and a height that kept the wire out of the way of anyone who passed by, "whether they be giraffes." The poles were spaced precisely at twenty-five to the mile and buried at a depth that enabled the line to "withstand all storms."

Like most important technological advances, the telegraph soon became a fact of life in New Mexico. It doubtless made business and personal communications with the rest of the country easier. Certainly, it provided New Mexicans with the latest news from the nation and the world, providing an access to information which may have been even more important for its time than the much touted Internet communications of today.

Bibliographic Note: Arrival of the telegraph is announced in the *Santa Fe Daily New Mexican*, July 8, 1868. The subsequent 1872 description of the telegraph line is from *The Daily New Mexican*, September 28, 1876.

Squatters in the Palace

One of the most audacious actions in the history of Santa Fe was that of private citizens who felt they owned or had a right to reside in the Palace of the Governors. One of these individuals even sued the government for trying to evict him.

In January of 1883, David K. Osborn, an employee of the Texas, Santa Fe, and Northern Railroad "took and held armed possession" of a room in the Palace of the Governors. The room, which had been vacated by the Second National Bank that same day, was about twenty feet square and located in the northwestern corner of the building. None of the extant documentation explains why Osborn claimed a right to this room, but some sources felt that he attempted to exercise a type of "squatters' rights" as part of an elaborate plan by the Santa Fe Ring to prevent the United States Post Office from moving into the vacant space. When Osborn took over the space and moved his bed and furniture into the building, it allegedly prevented the cancellation of a post office rental contract held by an unnamed member of the Santa Fe Ring.

In April 1883, the government apparently took action to eject Osborn from the building. Osborn responded by filing suit against the federal government, claiming their actions were illegal and sought damages of $1,000! A jury trial in U.S. District Court found for the government and fined Osborn

$75.00, but an obstinate Osborn appealed the decision. His challenge was based on the premise that several members of the jury were aware by hearsay alone that the Palace was government property. In January 1885, the New Mexico Supreme Court ruled that Osborn was right and that the government had failed to prove it in fact owned the building. Osborn was allowed a new trial.

There is no indication that the new trial was ever held. Instead, the government and Osborn apparently reached some type of agreement and nothing else is heard of him. However, the issue of squatters in the Palace continued because the man representing Osborn, attorney William Breeden, was himself a squatter in the Palace. The offices in which he and his brother, Marshall A. Breeden, conducted both official business and their private law practice were located in rooms adjacent to the governor's office.

William Breeden presents an interesting case in the study of territorial politics. Ralph Emerson Twitchell described him as "the shrewdest politician and most capable lawyer of his time." These are strong words, considering that Breeden was a close associate of Thomas B. Catron, the man generally considered to have been the principal leader of the infamous "Santa Fe Ring" of that period. Breeden also held the position of Attorney General for New Mexico for a number of years during the 1870s and 1880s. Marshall Breeden, his brother, served as Assistant Attorney General for much of that period. Breeden actually held the office of New Mexico Attorney General while he represented David Osborn in his suit against the federal government!

Breeden's political clout can be illustrated by the attempts of Governor Edmund G. Ross to remove him from office. In late 1885, Governor Ross, a sworn enemy of the Santa Fe Ring, suspended Breeden as Attorney General, alleging he interfered with Ross's attempts to reform territorial government and reduce the power of "The Ring." The suspension sparked a political and legal battle that Ross was unable to win. Breeden's broad political support and a law that limited the governor's ability to fill vacancies without legislative confirmation, allowed Breeden to remain in office for most of Governor Ross's term.

In 1889, however, the federal government was vigorously researching the status of the venerable Palace of the Governors. Among the findings reported by the Department of the Interior was that Breeden's use of several rooms in the building for a private law office made him "an intruder" who should be evicted. These reports note Breeden claimed ownership because he had purchased the "right" to use the rooms from former U.S. Attorney Thomas B. Catron nearly twenty years earlier. He claimed Catron had spent several hundred dollars of his own money to repair the rooms and when Breeden was appointed Attorney General in 1872, he paid Catron the cost of these improvements and received the right to occupy them "for the performance of his official duties."

As of 1890, however, Breeden held no official position with the territorial government but continued to occupy his former offices in the palace for the use of his private law practice. For more than fifteen years, no one had publicly questioned his right to be there, much less attempted to evict him. In early 1891, a persistent federal government finally convinced William Breeden to vacate the rooms in which he had practiced law for nearly two decades, thus ending the strange saga of squatters in the Palace of the Governors.

—◆—

Bibliographic Note: Numerous documents related to Osborn and Breeden's occupation of the Palace are in the Department of

Interior Territorial Papers, New Mexico, 1851–1914. National Archives Microfilm, Microcopy 364, Roll 4. *The Daily New Mexican*, November 14, 1885 and other issues of the period report on the controversy and legal actions surrounding the evictions.

UFOs Over Galisteo, 1880

Reports of Unidentified Flying Objects—UFOs—are front-page news. It is therefore quite easy to imagine that more than a century ago, when airplanes were not yet developed, a flying object of any kind would have been sensational news. So it must have been thus when the March 29, 1880, issue of the *Weekly New Mexican* reported "A Mysterious Aerial Phantom" was spotted flying across the sky near Galisteo southeast of Santa Fe.

The newspaper indicated several men had been walking near the railroad tracks at Galisteo Junction (present-day Lamy) the night of March 26, when they heard voices that seemed to come from the sky. At first, they thought it was an echo from someone talking in the nearby hills, but when they looked up, they saw a large flying object approach from the west. As the object approached, they were able to make out a gigantic balloon, shaped like a fish. It swooped low enough that the amazed observers could see distinct writing, or characters, on the side of the gondola that carried the passengers. "The air machine," they noted, "appeared to be entirely under the control of the occupants, and guided by a large sailing apparatus." It was "monstrous in size," and capable of carrying eight or ten persons. The observers were fascinated by the speed and maneuverability of the "air machine."

The occupants of the balloon seemed to be having a great time, as music, laughter, and voices in a language the men could not understand came from the vessel. Then suddenly, several objects were dropped from the balloon. In the darkness, however, the men found only "a magnificent flower, with a slip of exceedingly fine silk like paper," on which were written some characters that resembled Japanese. Then the vessel "assumed a great height and moved off very rapidly towards the east."

At first light the following morning, a diligent search for other objects dropped from the balloon uncovered a cup "of very peculiar workmanship," and very different from anything the men had ever seen. Both the cup and the flower they found the night before, were reported on display at Galisteo Junction, where they could be examined "by anyone who desire[d] to see them."

The paper also reported that the following day, a "collector of curiosities" had gone to see the flower and cup. The unnamed collector was so amazed by the objects dropped from the balloon that he offered "such a sum of money for them that it could not be refused." The new owner of the puzzling artifacts then proceeded to express his opinion that the balloon was undoubtedly from Asia, most likely, he noted, "from Jedde."

Nothing else was heard about the incident until a few days later, when the newspaper published an extraordinary explanation to the mystery of the balloon and objects that had been dropped from the aerial apparition. "Solved at Last," headlined the paper, "The Explanation of the Baloon [sic] Mystery which has been perplexing Galisteo." The paper proceeded to explain that the unidentified individual who bought the flower and cup had been "excavating for ancient curiosities" at the old Pecos Pueblo church, when a group of tourists stopped by to visit him.

Among the tourists was a "wealthy young Chinaman" who was touring the wild west. The group was shown the objects, and their attention was drawn to the writing on the wrapping of the flower that had been dropped from the balloon. When the young man from China saw the writings, he shouted for joy, and exclaimed that he knew who had dropped the objects!

He explained that for some years, China had held "great interest" on the subject of aerial navigation. Large investments had produced experimental aircraft shortly before he had left Peking, and "strong hopes were expressed that victory had at last crowned these efforts." The visitor opined that the "mysterious aerial phantom" was in fact "the first of a regular line of communication between the Celestial Empire and America."

The young man further explained that when he left China, he had been engaged to marry a young lady from a very wealthy family. His fiancée, who had a sister who lived in New York, was apparently aboard the balloon. Knowing he was in this part of the country, she must have written the note, placed it in the cup, and dropped it overboard, hoping, as it did, that the message would find its way to him. The visitor from China was reportedly last seen boarding the train and headed to New York, confident his fiancée would be awaiting him when he arrived. A happy and fitting explanation to "Galisteo's Apparition."

A far-fetched story? Of course. But in retrospect, no more unbelievable than contemporary reports of UFOs that are represented as being from other worlds. Our ancestors, like many of us today, also looked up into the skies and wondered.

⸺◈⸺

Bibliographic Note: This nineteenth-century UFO was reported in The *Weekly New Mexican*, March 29, 1880. Subsequent issues provided the follow-up explanation.

The Circus Comes to Town

Mas antes, few events caused a greater stir in communities than news that the circus was coming to town! Several weeks before the circus arrived, front men created great excitement about the coming attractions by papering communities along the travel route with enticing posters and buying elaborate advertisements in local newspapers.

So it was in Santa Fe when "W. W. Cole's New Colossal Shows Consolidated Three-Ring Circus" came through New Mexico in 1884. An enticing, two-column ad in the *Santa Fe New Mexican Review* ran daily for more than two weeks before the show was scheduled to arrive on October 8. For the admission price of one dollar (fifty cents for children under ten), the audience was assured they would "behold the world's greatest wonders." One could enjoy the spectacle from reserved, cushioned opera chairs that were available at a slightly higher price.

The newspaper noted that an effort had been made to arrange a special reduced price for school children, but circus management could not agree due to the high transportation costs and other expenses in the West. Most school children, however, did get a holiday, and the general feeling was that they would have a good time and benefit greatly from the lessons they could learn about "humanity and zoology."

Under the "largest tent ever used," they could anticipate a menagerie of performing and exotic display animals such as elephants, camels, kangaroos, ostriches, and a "snow white buffalo." Human performers included twelve "genuine Bedouin Arabs" as well as a "human fly" and an exotic female snake charmer. "Blondine, the Austrian rope walker" and several "tattooed South Sea savages" were among the 5,000 promised attractions.

A huge and enthusiastic crowd greeted the circus train Wednesday morning, October 8. A "sea of expectant faces" lined the route along San Francisco Street as the parade made its way to the plaza at the center of town and then south across the river to an open area near the railroad depot. The newspaper reported the scene was reminiscent of "one of those mystical pilgrimages to Mecca with their gorgeous solemnity, bright colorings, and so many dark, interesting faces." Everyone agreed it was the best parade they had ever seen.

The circus itself consisted of the main tent and two smaller "menagerie tents" where "nearly every species of animal creation known to zoology" were displayed. A white hippopotamus, reportedly purchased by W. W. Cole for the princely sum of $50,000, drew special attention from the spectators, but the numerous displays of snakes, lions, and other seldom-seen animals also attracted their share of awe and admiration. Promised "monster reptiles," however, were missing because they had died in Leadville, Colorado. Other displays featured wax statues of "presidents, financial kings, and crowned heads." Among them was a full-size representation of President Chester A. Arthur, which the newspaper quipped, resembled Dr. William Eggert, a Santa Fe physician!

The show itself consisted of two performances, the first at about one o'clock in the afternoon, and the second later that evening. Although the afternoon show was judged the better of the two, both performances apparently lived up to their billing. "Space fails to tell of the splendors of the arenic display," noted the reporter,

> beginning with its magnificent entree, a superb kaleidoscope . . . of bright color and ever changing effects, and leading up to the most marvelous exhibitions of skill, of grace, of wondrous strength and daring, by leapers, acrobats, tumblers, dashing and fearless bareback riders, trapeze performers, wire walkers, jugglers, bicyclists, roller skaters, Greco-Roman posturers, and equestrians.

The skills demonstrated by the various equestrian troupes apparently impressed everyone the most. These acts, noted the reporter, "rouse the spectators to the highest pitch of excitement." One cannot help but wonder if these might have prompted a few star-struck youngsters to try and coax a trick or two from "old Nellie" when they returned home.

It seems that nearly everyone got their money's worth. However, despite the large crowds, circus management claimed they were losing money in New Mexico, and were pleased to be on their way to closing the season and spending the winter in St. Louis. "Strange as it may seem," a circus official lamented, "the native people are not enthusiastic circus patrons." Although the circus itself may have lost money, Santa Fe merchants were clearly pleased with the business generated by the crowds which came to "see the elephant." Butchers, bakers, grain dealers, hotels, filigree jewelers, and curiosity shops were reportedly "overrun with patrons all day." Amazing how even in the old days, the success of a public event was measured by the amount of business it generated.

Bibliographic Note: The principal report of the circus perform-ances is from the *Santa Fe New Mexican Review*, October 8, 1884. The advertisements are from issues subsequent to that date.

Early Hotels and Restaurants in New Mexico

When we travel, one of our principal concerns is finding places to eat and spend the night. These same concerns were undoubtedly on the minds of travelers in the "good old days." *Mas antes*, however, travelers usually carried their own bedding and food, while others obtained *posada* (lodging) with relatives and friends en route or when they arrived at their destination.

Although travelers of 150 years ago did not have the choices available to modern travelers, commercial lodging and board were available in Santa Fe and other towns in New Mexico. One of the earliest hotels in Santa Fe opened almost immediately after the American occupation in August 1846. That same month, Benjamin Pruett was reported operating what one young army officer called "the only hotel in the place." Pruett reportedly set "a respectable table," which included welcome condiments such as pepper and mustard.

By 1847, Santa Fe boasted at least two hotels. The "Missouri House," owned by Nicolas Pino and John Abel, was located along the main street of the city. In addition to accommodations, they offered "the rarest and best served dishes of the season," as well as "the choicest liquors." Their advertisement in the September 17, 1847 issue of the *Santa Fe Republican*, claimed that the owners had nearly completed a "splendid ballroom" which would be "far superior" to any other in the city.

The main competition of the Missouri House was the "Santa Fe House," which advertised "Breakfast, Dinner or Supper [at] any hour of the day or night, cooked in Mexican or American fashion." W. W. Amos, the proprietor, also offered a private room for club meetings, a service that included a "servant" in constant attendance. By August 1848, the "Santa Fe House" was bought out by A. M. Copeland, and renamed the "Independence House."

Similar places of business were established in other towns throughout New Mexico. By 1848, advertisements for the "Taos Hotel" boasted of its "many large and ventilated rooms for transient or permanent boarders." They offered moderate prices and meals consisting of "the very best the market can afford."

In Albuquerque, an early hotel was operated by two men who purchased a large private house and converted it into a commercial establishment. They promised to spare no effort to provide their customers with "comfortable and well prepared fare." The best hotels of this period also offered convenient stables, corrals, and feed for their customers' horses.

One of the most famous of these early establishments was the "Exchange Hotel." The Exchange had its beginnings as the "United States Hotel," which was established in late 1847 on the southeast corner of the plaza in Santa Fe. That December, the "United States Hotel" was the subject of what may be New Mexico's first newspaper restaurant review. That month, editors of the *Santa Fe Republican* had dinner there and reported their impression of the attentive service and "numerous dishes" placed before them.

By 1850, however, the "United States Hotel" had changed owners and been renamed the "Exchange Hotel." The new establishment seems to have quickly become very popular. In October 1850, a "public dinner" was held there in honor of

Hugh N. Smith, New Mexico's recently elected delegate to the United States Congress. When the Exchange hosted a similar dinner for Judge Perry E. Brocchus in 1855, the service and food were described as "most elegant and brilliant. . .and well calculated to grace the occasion and to do credit to the excellent house at which it was prepared."

During the following decades, numerous hotels and restaurants came and went, but the Exchange persisted. The August 5, 1872 issue of *The Daily New Mexican* devoted an entire column to a story on the Exchange restaurant. The editors apparently dined there regularly and had become curious about what went into the preparation of their "daily hash." They decided to investigate further and planned to spring a surprise visit to the "cooking department" of the hotel. They seemed surprised to find "everything in the most complete order; the floors just scrubbed, nothing out of place, neatness and cleanliness on every side, everybody working as if he knew just what he was about." Thomas McDonald, the proprietor, allowed them a full tour, which included the store rooms where the fresh meat and groceries were kept. The kitchen itself was judged to have been "a model of cleanliness."

The room the reporters were most anxious to visit, however, was where the hotel stored its supply of wine and liquors. Once inside the warehouse where these were kept, they offered their services as tasters, and judging by the jolly and loquacious conclusion of their report, they apparently spent a significant portion of their visit at this location.

The Exchange Hotel continued in business at this location for a number of years. However, by the early 1900s the building had deteriorated, and the site was eventually cleared soon after World War I. La Fonda was later built on this same location, continuing a long tradition of hospitality at this historic corner at the end of the Santa Fe Trail.

———◆———

Bibliographic Note: Information on the early hotels and restaurants are from the *Santa Fe Republican*, September 17, 1847 and other issues of the period.

PART FIVE

Biography

This final section of stories from the archives concentrates on the lives of a few interesting people who lived in nineteenth-century New Mexico. These stories do not pretend to be extensive life histories, but rather, they serve to provide a few of the "forgotten people" of our history a modicum of recognition. One of these individuals, Manuel Armijo, had a long and distinguished career and is well-known in the annals of our history. Unfortunately, much of what has been written about him is derisive and often based on unreliable secondary sources. His life, as that of J. Francisco Chaves, another of our subjects in this section, awaits a full biography. The remaining stories touch on the lives of a career soldier and public servant, a frontier scout, a fascinating trouble-maker, a troubled businessman, and a young girl. Unlike Armijo and Chaves, these persons are generally unknown or barely mentioned in our written history. In this section, we piece together a few elements of their lives through the often barely perceptible voices they left behind so that their role in our history, however minute, will not be forgotten.

A Soldier's Career

More often than any of us would like to admit, even veteran researchers get sidetracked from projects by a few words or lines in a document that have nothing to do with what one is looking for at the moment. This story is the result of one such distraction, one that became more interesting as I looked beyond the simple document that initially drew my attention.

While reviewing microfilm of the Mexican Archives of New Mexico, my attention was drawn to a slip of paper in the military records of the *presidio* company of Santa Fe. This seemingly insignificant piece of paper, dated April 12, 1834, is a simple request by the *cabo* (approximate rank of a corporal) Antonio Sena, in which he asks for an advance of six pesos on his salary of 25 pesos a month. His wife had recently given birth and Sena wanted to purchase some items for her medical care. Blas de Hinojos, the company commander, approved the advance in the amount of five pesos and troop accounts show Sena was given the cash that same day.

Curiosity about whether I could find a record of baptism for the child Sena alluded to in the request led me to a search through some of the records of the Archdiocese of Santa Fe for the period. I did not find the child's baptismal record, but in the process of that search, I found that Sena himself was baptized in Santa Fe on March 19, 1809. He was the son of

José Manuel de Jesús Sena and María Josefa Madrid. His service record shows that on June 10, 1829, at the age of twenty, Sena entered military service with the *"Compania permanente de Santa Fe."* He held the rank of *soldado*, or private, for little more than three and a half years before being promoted to *cabo* in 1832. During this period he married María del Refugio Ortiz from Santa Cruz de la Cañada. The infant Sena referred to in his 1834 request was presumably the result of his marriage to María del Refugio.

At the point that I had uncovered much of Sena's personal life, I was once again distracted by his service record. Service records are one of the little-known treasures of our Mexican Archives of New Mexico. This collection contains hundreds of documents pertaining to individual soldiers who served in the military during New Mexico's Mexican period (1821–1846). As it turns out, the records pertaining to Antonio Sena are extraordinarily complete and tell us not only about the man, but also about that period of our history.

Some of the most interesting of Sena's records are the numerous *"hojas de servicio"* which detail his entire career from the time he enlisted in 1829 through his rise to the rank of captain in 1842. These include his promotions to *cabo* in 1832, to *Sargento* in 1836, *Alférez Segundo* in 1839, *Alférez Primero* in 1841, and finally, to *Capitán* in 1842. They also show he participated in at least three major Indian campaigns. The first of these occurred within four months of his enlistment while escorting a commercial caravan traveling from Santa Fe to the United States. On October 6, 1829, he took part in a skirmish with the Pawnee near the Cimarron River. He also took part in campaigns against the Navajo in 1834 and 1835.

Sena also participated in two battles during the northern New Mexico insurrection known as the Revolt of 1837. Then-*sargento* Sena was part of the contingent of troops sent from

Excerpt of Antonio Sena's service record shows the progression of his military career. MANM: 1844 Military Records.

Santa Fe to suppress the rebellion centered in Santa Cruz de la Cañada and Chimayó. The reports indicate Sena was captured by the rebels during a desperate battle with the "*Cañaderos*" on August 8, 1837. However, he was apparently released or escaped because he participated in the subsequent January 1838 battle in which the insurrection was defeated. One cannot help but wonder if his sense of duty to the Mexican Republic may have matched him against some of his relatives on the battlefield. His wife, after all, was from Santa Cruz de la Cañada, a rebel stronghold.

Sena's long military record, however, is crowned by his actions during the Texas invasion of New Mexico in 1841. In recognition of his service against the "*aventureros Tejanos*," Manuel Armijo, his commanding officer and governor of New Mexico, recommended him for an "*escudo de honor*," the

Mexican equivalent of a Medal of Honor. This honor was granted to Sena by the president of the Republic of Mexico a few months later, along with his promotion to captain.

This brief look at the life of Antonio Sena shows his development from a raw recruit to a professional soldier and patriot of the Mexican republic. He had come a long way since his enlistment in 1829 and that day in 1834 when his concern for the welfare of his wife prompted him to request an advance on his salary—the simple piece of paper, that voice from the past, that drew my attention to his extraordinary career.

———◆———

Bibliographic Note: Antonio Sena's petition for funds is found in "Miscellaneous receipts," MANM: 1834 Military Records (18/1089). His military career is pieced together from numerous service records and reports found in the MANM military records and company accounts, 1829 through 1844. More information on these military records and Sena's public career can be found in Robert J. Tórrez, "Archives Reveal Presidio Treasure Trove," *La Herencia del Norte* (fall 2000): 24.

New Mexico's First Official Historian

I retired from my position as State Historian with the New Mexico State Records Center and Archives effective December 22, 2000. At that time, I had held the position of State Historian for thirteen-and-a-half years. I am proud to say that I probably held this position longer than any of the distinguished persons who had preceded me. At that time, I felt it was appropriate to utilize the December 2000 column of "Voices From the Past" to recognize the individuals who had preceded me in that position.

The position of State Historian has occasionally existed in state government only since 1946. That year, George Curry, who served as governor of New Mexico from 1907 through 1910, was the first person appointed with the title of "state historian." Curry served in that capacity from 1946 until his death in 1947. Interestingly, it was George Curry who originally appointed Ralph Emerson Twitchell to the territorial period equivalent of that position (although not with that title), when Curry was governor nearly half a century earlier.

There was no "official historian" in the territorial or state government between the time J. Francisco Chaves held the position in 1903–1904 or after George Curry died in 1947. The position was resurrected by the state legislature in 1967, when Myra Ellen Jenkins, whose name became synonymous with the position, was appointed State Historian.

Bust of J. Francisco Chaves at the New Mexico State Capitol.
Drawing by Vanessa Tórrez.

Dr. Jenkins retained the title until she retired in 1980. The following year, Hilario Romero was State Historian for a few months, followed by Stan Hordes (1981–1985), and then myself. It is possible that during this century some persons may have called themselves or been referred to by that title, but no one other than these five individuals have officially been recognized as the State Historian. I am proud to have served in such select company.

Some may argue that Gaspar Pérez de Villagrá, who published his *Historia de la Nueva México* in 1610, was New Mexico's first historian. However, it was J. Francisco Chaves who held the first official appointment to a position that approximates the contemporary State Historian. Chaves had a long and distinguished career of public service. Born in 1833 in the Los Padillas neighborhood of Albuquerque's south valley, Chaves counts among his many distinguished ancestors Francisco Xavier Chaves, who served as governor of New Mexico in 1822.

Chaves was educated at St. Louis University and the College of Physicians and Surgeons in New York. As a young man, he served in Navajo campaigns with Kit Carson, fought at Valverde during the Civil War, and attained the rank of colonel in the New Mexico Volunteers. During subsequent decades, he was admitted to the bar and served as district attorney for Valencia County. He was also elected the New Mexico territorial delegate to the U.S. Congress, and served numerous terms as a representative in the territorial legislature. One need not go further into his life to show he was one of nineteenth-century New Mexico's brightest and most dedicated public servants. When Chaves County was created in 1889, it was named in his honor.

In 1903, the territorial legislature passed an act "for the writing and publishing of the history of New Mexico" to be used as a textbook for the public schools. Chaves himself may have seen the need for such a textbook. That year he completed a term as the territory's Superintendent of Public Instruction and was immediately appointed to the task of preparing the history textbook. Archival documents show Chaves apparently worked on the book from early 1903 through much of 1904. During this period, he regularly submitted vouchers for his salary of $125 a month as "Territorial Historian and Clerk." These certify he was "actively engaged" in the collection of material for the book. However, Chaves's career as a historian was cut short by an assassin's bullet on November 27, 1904, at Pino's Well in Torrance County.

Chaves's killer was apparently never found. Neither were any manuscripts or materials he may have collected for his history textbook. In 1907, Governor George Curry wrote to Ralph Emerson Twitchell after hearing that Twitchell was interested in writing a history of New Mexico. Curry offered Twitchell the task begun by Chaves four years earlier, and as the saying goes, "the rest is history." During the next two decades, Twitchell produced his two volumes of the *Spanish Archives of New Mexico* and the five-volume set of *The Leading Facts of New Mexico History*. These have since become the standard by which all subsequent books on New Mexico history are measured. By his untimely death, J. Francisco Chaves, who was eulogized as "the historian of the territory," lost his opportunity to achieve what might have become his most enduring legacy—recognition as New Mexico's first "official historian."

Bibliographic Note: Information on Chaves can be found in the SRCA "Miscellaneous Records: Persons." A lengthy report of his death and biographical information is reported in *The Daily Citizen* (Albuquerque), November 28, 1904. The development of the position of New Mexico State Historian can be traced through the various volumes of *Law of New Mexico*, Chapter 23 (1903), Chapter 63 (1945), Chapter 18 (1947), and Chapter 7 (1967). Details on George Curry's term as State Historian can be found in H. B. Hening, ed. *George Curry 1861–1947, An Autobiography* (Albuquerque: University of New Mexico Press, 1958).

Tomás Chacón, Frontier Scout and Pioneer

One of the tragedies and ironies of the way history is written is that we seldom hear much about the real frontiersmen who did so much to make New Mexico the fascinating place it is today. If you look through the shelves of books and articles on scouts and so-called frontiersmen, you will probably not find the name of Tomás Chacón. Yet, numerous documents and reports of the period show that for more than three decades, he was one of northern New Mexico's most sought-after interpreters and guides.

We know little about Chacón's early life. The records of Abiquiú baptisms show one Tomás de Jesús Chacón was baptized on December 23, 1793, the son of José Antonio Chacón and María Juana Guadalupe Archuleta. If this baptismal record is the correct one for the Tomás Chacón of frontier New Mexico fame, then it is likely he is the same person listed in the 1850 United States census for Rio Arriba County at age 59 with his wife María and three children.

During his life along the rugged frontier of northwestern New Mexico, Tomás Chacón developed an intimate relationship with the Utes of that region. That relationship and his role in society is reflected in the baptism records of Santo Tomás Apostol de Abiquiú. Between 1832 and 1841, there are at least eight baptisms of Ute children listed as "servants of Tomás Chacón." This clearly indicates that he, like many of his neighbors, was deeply involved in the trade and raising of *cautivos*, captive Indian children, that was so prevalent in New Mexico at that time.

Chacón begins to show up frequently in the contemporary historical record in 1850. That year, he served as the guide and interpreter for the William Z. Angney expedition that traveled to California over the Old Spanish Trail. The journal of this expedition notes that his "intimate acquaintance with the [Ute territory] and its wild inhabitants and their language, [was] of no small service to us." Daniel Jones's book, *Forty Years Among the Indians*, chronicles this same journey. He credits "old Thomas" with seeing them through several "close calls" because he was always able to "talk the Indians into peace." Jones credits Chacón with saving his life on more than one occasion.

In 1851, Chacón is reported trading with the Indians along the San Juan River. That same year, he led the pursuit of a band of Jicarilla Apaches who raided Abiquiú and El Rito. His knowledge of their language was instrumental in securing the return of livestock the Jicarilla had stolen from the settlements.

Tomás Chacón also played a prominent role in the William F. M. Arny expedition that negotiated a treaty with the Utes at the San Juan River in 1868. Chacón not only served as the guide and interpreter for the expedition, but appears as one of the witnesses and signatories of the treaty Arny negotiated with the Utes. What may be best known about this 1868 expedition is the photograph taken of Arny with a group of Ute and Jicarilla leaders. The photograph shows Tomás Chacón peering from the back row between two Ute chiefs. A woodcut of that famous photograph that appeared in the August 22, 1868 issue of *Harper's Weekly* illustrates the earlier story of Sobita, the Ute chief.

The final entry I have found for Tomás Chacón is the service he provided as the interpreter for the U.S. Army when they attempted to negotiate an agreement with Sobita and his Capote band of Utes at Las Nutritas (present-day Tierra Amarilla) in 1872. When negotiations broke down, the commanding officer sent Chacón to talk to Sobita and convince him to return. One report indicates that this time, Chacón's powers of persuasion apparently failed. The angry Utes "horsewhipped" Chacón and sent him back to inform the troops that they wanted to fight. The pitched battle between the Utes and the United States cavalry that ensued eventually led to the capitulation of the Utes and their removal to a reservation in Colorado.

Tomás Chacón disappears from the historical record after 1872. If he was in fact born in 1793, Chacón was nearly eighty years old when called into this final service for the U.S. government. He did his duty, returned to his home in the Abiquiú region and quietly melted into undeserved anonymity. In his own time, Tomás Chacón was as well-known as any of the more famous personages of frontier New Mexico. I hope his descendants realize the important role he played in our history.

———— ◆ ————

Bibliographic Note: Chacón's life and colorful career is pieced together from dozens of sources, many found in the massive Records of the New Mexico Superintendancy of Indian Affairs, National Archives Microcopy T-21. His role in the Angney expedition of 1850 is found in the Daniel Jones book mentioned above as well as the extensive report of the expedition itself serialized in the *Daily Missouri Republican*, September 2, 1852 and subsequent issues. The baptism and marriage records of the Archdiocese of Santa Fe for the Abiquiú region are also a valuable source of information.

Governor Armijo's Medal of Honor

One of the defining moments of New Mexico's short tenure as a part of the Mexican republic came in 1841. That year, for reasons that are still a mystery to many of us, Texas President Mirabeau B. Lamar sent an armed expedition to New Mexico in hopes of opening trade between the Texas capital in Austin and Santa Fe. It also seems Lamar hoped to exercise the Texas claim that the Rio Grande was their western border and apparently felt there was some sentiment in New Mexico for becoming part of the Texas republic. Lamar could not have been more wrong. The expedition under General Hugh McLeod was badly equipped and organized. By the time they straggled into the settlements along New Mexico's eastern frontier, the Texans were starving and in disarray.

In the meantime, the New Mexican government under Manuel Armijo was advised that McLeod and his expedition were approaching the eastern New Mexico frontier. Governor Armijo was ordered to consider this an armed invasion by a country hostile to the Mexican republic. Armijo's forces were waiting for the scattered and bedraggled Texans, and by early September had rounded them up with little trouble. The news of Armijo's triumph over the Texans was quickly hailed as a great victory, not only for New Mexico, but for a beleaguered Mexican nation. A circular issued at El Paso del Norte on

September 28, 1841 joyfully trumpeted the defeat of the Texans. "*Viva la Patria*," it announced, "*Los tejanos han sido vencidos*" ("The Texans have been defeated").

This ill-fated incident, known as the "Texas-Santa Fe Expedition," was made infamous by George W. Kendall, one of the members of the expedition, in his two-volume *Narrative of the Texan Santa Fe Expedition*. However, our history books tell us little of what happened on the New Mexican side of the incident. For certain, the victory over the Texans provided a great lift for the morale of the Mexican republic and the events of that summer were greatly appreciated by the Mexican government. One of the little-known aspects of this incident is that almost as soon as the reports from New Mexico reached the capital in Mexico, the President ordered that Armijo and his officers be awarded "*una cruz de honor*," a medal honoring their service against the Texans.

These medals of honor have become a topic of some speculation and frustration. What did they look like? Who actually received them? And most importantly, what has become of them? Apparently, none of these important military awards have survived the past one hundred and fifty years.

The historical record indicates Manuel Armijo received his personal "*cruz de honor*" the morning of January 7, 1846. On January 12, 1846, Armijo wrote to government officials in Mexico and acknowledged he had received it along with a length of green ribbon that was evidently worn with the medal. Armijo's letters indicate he was justifiably proud of the medal. His correspondence of the previous four years included several reminders to his superiors that he had not yet received the medal authorized to him for his service against the Texans in 1841.

So what became of the medal? Is this medal of honor the one Armijo is shown wearing in the portrait of him found in Ralph Emerson Twitchell's *The History of the Military*

Manuel Armijo, possibly wearing his escudo de honor.
Ralph Emerson Twitchell, *The History of the Military
Occupation of New Mexico*, p. 55.

Occupation of New Mexico? Armijo is not wearing the medal in
his full-length portrait that is located at the Albuquerque
Museum. It seems that examples of these medals should have
surfaced because several officers of the *presidio* and militia
forces were also awarded the same *"cruz de honor."* My own
research as well as that of Geronimo Padilla and Charles
Martinez show that Captains Donaciano Vigil and Francisco
Martinez, Lieutenants Tomas Armijo and Antonio Sena,
Alférez Juan Lopez , and Sergeants Francisco de la Peña, Pedro
Sandoval, Lorenzo Tafoya, Ramon López, and José Tenorio

were also authorized to receive this distinctive honor. Additionally, at least one militia officer, the *Alférez* José Dolores Tafoya, was awarded a medal for his service in the 1841 Texas expedition.

So what has become of these symbols of New Mexico's singular triumph over the Texans? Have they all disappeared? Or is it possible that some families still retain these unique and valuable artifacts, unsure of what they are and unaware of the patriotism of their brave ancestors? Maybe one will surface in the future and we can all acknowledge the service these men performed for their country.

Bibliographic Note: This story is pieced together from dozens of documents found in the governor's correspondence in the Mexican Archives of New Mexico for the years 1842 through 1846. Specific acknowledgment that Governor Manuel Armijo and some of his troops were to be awarded this "*cruz de honor*" is found in Armijo's letter to the Misisterio de Guerra y Marina, January 11, 1842. January 9, 1841–January 13, 1842, "Letterbook of communications sent to Ministerio de Guerra y Marina." MANM: 1841 Governor's Papers (28/1459). Mention of the award also appears in the service records of the individuals listed. The Mexican response to the capture of the Texans is found in a broadside published in Chihuahua, September 28, 1841, University of Arizona Special Collections Library: Mexican Broadsides, #0047. Governor Armijo's portrait is from Ralph Emerson Twitchell, *The History of the Military Occupation of the Territory of New Mexico From 1846 to 1851 by the Governement of the United States* (Chicago: The Rio Grande Press, Inc., 1963): 55.

"... nothing but trouble ..."

In this series of stories, I have often noted how history generally consists of the lives of those who are famous, powerful, and important. As a consequence, we normally do not hear about the little known, but nonetheless interesting people that make the study of history such a fascinating subject.

One such person was Andrew P. Morris, a feisty individual who showed up in New Mexico sometime in the 1880s and quickly became a thorn in the side of some of the most powerful and influential men in New Mexico. Morris first appears in the historical record in 1890. That year, Rio Arriba County court records show he pleaded guilty to cutting the fences of one Edward A. Varburg near Amargo, located west of the northern New Mexico railroad town of Chama. He was fined five dollars plus court costs and placed under bond not to repeat the offense. There is no indication he cut any more fences, but Morris subsequently ended up getting into more than his fair share of trouble. During the decade that followed, he was convicted of an assault, served a two year sentence in the territorial penitentiary, and found himself embroiled in one of the most notorious murder trials in New Mexico history.

Andrew P. Morris was not an imposing individual. The description in the penitentiary records show that in 1895, he was thirty-five years old, just over five feet, five inches tall, and weighed 134 pounds. His right leg was amputated just below

Andrew P. Morris. Penitentiary of New Mexico,
#908, NMSRCA.

the knee and he was missing parts of the second and third
fingers of his left hand. His mug shot shows a husky black man
with an impish smile that may reflect the feisty nature that got
him into so much trouble. Close examination of the photograph shows a handkerchief is draped over his left hand, presumably to hide its deformities. Other records hint he may
have been a native of Cuba.

Morris's long history of troubles apparently began when he
filed for a homestead in northwestern New Mexico in 1890.
He immediately ran into trouble with powerful men who con-
trolled the railroad and timber interests in that region.
According to Morris's letters, the lumber companies wanted

the timber from his land and the railroad wanted the land itself. The trouble he got into with Edward Varburg and the charges filed against him in 1890 apparently stemmed from this dispute. Then in 1894, he shot and wounded two men he claimed were illegally trying to evict him. For this incident, he was convicted of "assault with a deadly weapon" in late 1895 and sentenced to two years in the territorial penitentiary. The mug shot accompanying this story was taken at that time.

While he was awaiting trail between the time of his arrest in 1894 and his conviction more than a year later, he inundated government officials with letters about his situation. During this period, he contacted Thomas B. Catron and charged that Santa Fe District Attorney Jacob H. Crist and other officials were trying to coerce him and other prisoners held at the Santa Fe County jail to testify falsely in the infamous and politically charged trial of the Borrego brothers and their accomplices for the murder of former Santa Fe County Sheriff Francisco Chavez.

Even his time in prison did not go quietly. He served the full two-year sentence, possibly because he got into trouble several times. The penitentiary "Punishment Record Book" shows he was confined in a "dark cell" for periods of two to three days on at least four occasions. His offenses ranged from "back talk and insolence" to "possessing ink, pen and pencil without permission."

After he was released from prison in late 1897, Morris resumed his correspondence with public officials. He sought a pardon and restoration of his citizenship and asked Catron and Attorney General Edward L. Bartlett to look into what had happened to his land in Rio Arriba. Bartlett's response to Morris in April 1898 shows they were tired of dealing with him. Bartlett suggested it would be a good idea if Morris stayed away from Rio Arriba for a while. "You will have nothing but trouble there," he advised, "anywhere else you will stand a better show to live longer."

Morris apparently took Bartlett's advice and kept a low profile for a few years. However, he did not remain quiet forever. In 1906 he wrote to Governor Herbert J. Hagerman from the Puertocito ranch near Cerrillos and complained vigorously about the activities of one Antonio J. Ortiz and his "gang." The record does not show the outcome of these complaints, but his final letter does reflect an important aspect of this fascinating, if troublesome, individual. All he wanted, he claimed, was the opportunity to "make an honest living, which for a one legged man, I find hard enough to do." Clearly, Andrew P. Morris was an ordinary person with a highly developed sense of justice. While some of his search for that justice may have been misdirected, he vigorously confronted those that he felt kept him from attaining his goal of an honest living.

Bibliographic Note: Morris's difficulties with the law can be traced through the Rio Arriba County Criminal Cases nos. 927, 928, 1066 and 1067. His photograph and prison record are found in the Records of the Penitentiary of New Mexico, PNM #908. His correspondence with public officials is scattered through the letters received and sent of Governor Herbert J. Hagerman, 1906–1907; Records of the Attorney General, 1890–1912, and Edward Bartlett Papers, Political Correspondence, 1890–1892. All are found in the Territorial Archives of New Mexico. Additional correspondence is in the Thomas B. Catron Papers, University of New Mexico Special Collections, PC29.

The President of New Mexico

Many of the individuals who came to New Mexico along the Santa Fe Trail in the nineteenth century made positive and important contributions to the fascinating story of our state. Few, however, created a greater stir than a French Canadian entrepreneur and merchant named Joseph Mercure. Joseph Mercure and his younger brother Henry came to New Mexico along the Santa Fe Trail in the late 1840s. Their earliest mention is a listing that shows them as clerks in a St. Louis store in 1847. However, by the following year, the brothers had been issued a commercial license in Santa Fe under the soon-to-become familiar business name of *"J & H Mercure."*

In 1850, Joseph, age 32, and Henry, age 28, are listed in the United States census as residents of Santa Fe. By this time they were active in the Santa Fe Trail trade and had gone into business with other prominent individuals. Their enterprises included partnerships with Christopher "Kit" Carson, the famous scout. In the early 1850s, they shipped thousands of sheep to California over the Old Spanish Trail.

The extant records do not make it clear if the Mercure brothers were good businessmen, but their commercial ventures and travels brought them into contact with many colorful characters of the era. Joseph's acquaintance with one of these, a storekeeper named Peter Mullen, nearly cost him his life. In late October of 1851, Joseph Mercure was visiting with

Mullen in a corral located at the rear of Mullen's store. Mercure noticed an opened cask of gunpowder and that Mullen was waving a lighted cigar perilously close to the exposed powder. When Mercure suggested that Mullen was tempting fate and risking their lives, Mullen laughed and remarked that they were in no danger. To prove his point, Mullen foolishly touched the lighted cigar to the exposed powder. According to the newspaper report of this incident, Mercure, who apparently possessed "an instinct becoming a sensible man," attempted to jump to safety as soon as he saw Mullen make this foolhardy move. The ensuing explosion knocked both men to the ground. When the smoke cleared, Mullen found he had injured his right hand, the one that had held the offending cigar. Except for some superficial burns, scorched clothing, and singed beards, they had both miraculously escaped other serious injury, considering their proximity to the explosion of eighteen pounds of the volatile powder. The newspaper report of the incident sarcastically remarked that Mullen should heretofore test the "explosive properties of gunpowder . . . on a smaller scale."

Joseph Mercure next shows up in the public records as an eyewitness to the fatal encounter between Francis X. Aubrey and Richard H. Weightman in 1854. In August of that year, an argument between Aubrey and Weightman broke out in the Mercure store, located on the south side of the Santa Fe plaza. In the ensuing struggle, Weightman fatally stabbed Aubrey. Weightman was later indicted for murder but acquitted at his trial.

The Mercure brothers continued in business for several years. They also became involved in the exploration and prospecting of southwestern Colorado in the region where Durango and Silverton are located today. However, Joseph's mental state changed dramatically after their mining enterprises failed and Confederate forces occupied Santa Fe and sacked their store in April 1862. Records show they lost several hundred dollars' worth of clothing and merchandise.

That summer Joseph apparently began to experience hallucinations and demonstrate bizarre behavior. He claimed to have invented a "solar compass" that was going to make him a rich man and that he had discovered gold and diamond mines that would make Santa Fe the largest and wealthiest city in the country. He then declared New Mexico an independent state, proclaimed himself president of this new republic and began to issue verbal and written orders to civil and military authorities. When his orders were naturally ignored, he reacted angrily and became violent. The last straw came when Joseph assaulted a military officer who had refused to carry out his orders. Finally, it was decided to confine him before he injured himself or others, and Henry arranged to send his older brother to an asylum in the East for treatment. Joseph did not survive the trip. Sometime in September or October 1863, he died along the road to Missouri. He was buried along the banks of the Arkansas River, not far from the same Santa Fe Trail that had brought him to New Mexico two decades earlier.

Later that fall, Henry had the body of his brother exhumed and the remains returned to Santa Fe for a proper burial. When Joseph Mercure was buried in Santa Fe in mid-November 1863, the newspaper report of his funeral described the ceremonies as "grand and solemn." Ceremonies that perhaps befitted the first and only "president of New Mexico."

⟹•⟸

Bibliographic Note: Joseph Mercure's business dealings can be traced through the licenses issued to him and his brother Henry in the records of the Santa Fe County Sheriff and

Collector License Fees, 1847–1867, found at SRCA. Additional business dealings are found in the Manuel Alvarez Papers, University of New Mexico Special Collections. His experience with the exploding gunpowder is from the *Missouri Republican*, December 7, 1851. Details of his mental status and death are from the *Santa Fe Weekly Gazette*, August 15, September 5, and November 14, 1863. A brief story of Joseph Mercure's bout with insanity and death was J. Robert Jones, "The President in Santa Fe," *New Mexico Magazine* 29:1 (January 1951): 17.

Memoirs of a Young Girl

In 1996, I had the good fortune of meeting Mrs. Noel Brusman of Chicago at an Elderhostel held at Plaza Resolana in Santa Fe. Mrs. Brusman happened to mention that her grandmother, Lucena Alfintri Marcil had spent part of her childhood at Camp Good Hope, a mining town located in northern New Mexico west of Taos. Ena, as Ms. Marcil was affectionately known to her family, also happened to leave behind a memoir that detailed her recollections of life in the short-lived mining camp. These memoirs are a voice from the past that provide us with an intimate and rare glimpse of the experiences of a young girl in northern New Mexico more than a century ago.

Ena was born on February 22, 1873, in Matoon, Illinois. Her father, Alexis Marcil, was a French Canadian who enlisted in the Union army at age fourteen and fought in the Civil War. Ena's recollections of New Mexico begin in 1881, when her father and an uncle decided to try their luck at the recently discovered gold diggings at Good Hope, a site now known as Hopewell, located a few miles west of Taos and present-day Tres Piedras. Mr. Marcil built a log cabin there and sent to Kansas for his family. Ena recalls that when they arrived at Good Hope, her mother was the only woman in the mining town. She recalls the place as "a lively camp—a small store, saloon, assay office and a lot of miners living in cabins and a small mill . . . nearby."

Ena Marcil and her brothers, Ernest and Alexis, 1885.
Courtesy of Noel Brusman, author's collection.

Ena's memoir provides us with a rare personal look at life in a northern New Mexico mining town in the 1880s. She described hydraulic mining, which utilized a stream of pressurized water to loosen topsoil. The liquefied soil was then channeled into sluice boxes that had slats and holes along the bottom to catch the gold. She recalls seeing "good sized nuggets," one of which was worth eighteen dollars.

Ena also recalls several incidents that would have been typical of the violence that often characterized these mining towns. One of these involved a posse of more than fifty mounted and heavily armed men that arrived suddenly at the Marcil home in search of an unknown fugitive. On another occasion, Ena and her siblings watched from their window as another posse coaxed a young man to reveal where some stolen horses had been hidden. "He was driven under one of the trees, a rope tied around his neck and thrown over the limb of the tree while the men talked to him," Ena wrote. The rope was progressively tightened until he agreed to reveal the location of the stolen horses. Ena was justifiably relieved that she did not end up a witness to a frontier lynching.

Ena's recollections of New Mexico are not limited to the unpleasant realities of a rough frontier town. She was about eight years old when she and her family arrived at Good Hope in 1881, so naturally, there was plenty of time and opportunity to participate in the simple pleasures of childhood. She fondly recalls roving the surrounding hills with her siblings and other children. They climbed trees and played in the meadows while burros grazed and rested from their arduous task of transporting equipment and goods between the mines and the train station at Tres Piedras. They sometimes caught one of the tamer burros and tried to ride, but she notes, they "were usually thrown off." They also fished in a nearby stream using a bent pin tied to a string fastened to a rude pole. They had no trouble getting the fish to bite, she recalls, "but the pin wouldn't hold them," so they did not land the fish as often as she hoped.

Then there was the time the mother of one of their playmates made donuts. Ena had never seen such a marvelous item, made more interesting and mysterious by the fact that the boy often took a donut with him when they went fishing. "[W]hile he fished," she recalls, "he kept reaching in his pocket for a piece of donut, never offering a bite. I was so impressed, I made up my mind, if I could get a donut and go fishing, it would be the realization of my happiest dream!" Ena does not mention the name of the woman who created this marvelous confection, but one cannot help but wonder if there was a Mrs. Duncan living at Good Hope at that time.

In 1884, the Marcil family left Good Hope for Alamosa, Colorado, so that Ena and her brothers could attend school. That summer they loaded a covered wagon with their belongings and departed from New Mexico permanently. The accompanying photo of Ena and her brothers was taken on July 8, 1885 while they lived in Alamosa.

———•••———

Bibliographic Note: Ena Marcil's memoirs are courtesy of the manuscript in possession of Mrs. Noel Brusman.

Glossary of Spanish Terms

One of the most difficult and frustrating elements of reading old documents from the Spanish- and Mexican-period archives of New Mexico is trying to figure out the meaning of words that are seldom used in contemporary Spanish. During my research into these periods, I have developed a file of interesting words or terms and kept notes on the manner or context in which they were used. Many are archaic terms taken from documents produced by individuals responsible for documenting the administration of the Spanish colonial judicial and penal systems. This brief glossary consists of a selection of these words in the hope that readers will find them interesting and useful in their own research. Each definition will provide a context in which the word was used.

Aldabón: A handle or a grip, such as that on a door. It may also refer to a large handle on a container such as a strongbox. In 1801, for example, Martín de Yrigoyen was paid two reales for repairs to the *aldabón* of the door or gate of the *muralla*, or wall that surrounded the old military complex in Santa Fe.

Amacia: A form of *amación*, which refers to a deep and passionate love or affection. The *amacia* would therefore be the object of that affection, such as a girlfriend or lover. In 1846, Governor Manuel Armijo issued an order that *amacias* would no longer be allowed to receive or be issued a soldier's pay or commissary goods on behalf of that soldier. The soldiers would be required to pick up their pay personally. Soldiers in uniform were also prohibited from walking along the streets with a girlfriend on their arm.

Amansebo, amansebado: Concubinage or co-habitation; the act of living together outside marriage. Adultery was a crime in colonial Spain (as it still is in many parts of the world). Offenders were not necessarily sought out and prosecuted vigorously by Spanish officials, but if a couple's actions were blatant and a complaint was made, local officials found it necessary to act. Sometimes, a sexual relationship outside marriage is referred to in these documents as *amistad ilicita*. In 1701, for example, Agustin Saez and Luisa Barela, both of Santa Fe (and both married to someone else), were charged with co-habiting despite having been previously warned to discontinue their relationship. They not only persisted, but did so publicly, prompting formal charges that found the couple was not only living in sin, but causing serious public scandal. Luisa was ordered to leave Santa Fe and live with her brother and sister in Bernalillo. She was also warned not to try and sneak back to the capital. Saez was fined forty pesos and told to go back to his wife and live with her "as a husband." He was also warned that if he did not comply, he too, would be exiled.

Amonestar: An admonition or reprimand, usually combined with a graphic warning of the punishment that would be imposed if certain behavior persisted. In 1799, for example, Joseph Mariano Dominguez and Antonio Mondragon were released from custody following an investigation into their role in the murder of Juana de la Cruz Pacheco. The file is incomplete, but it seems that although they were the principal suspects, no direct evidence was found to implicate them for the killing. They were released with a verbal reprimand. The term *apercevidos* or *apercevimiento* is sometimes used in a similar manner.

Aposento: Technically a room in an apartment or house. In a number of older documents it denotes a bedroom or a room in which a person slept. Typical usage is in the statement made by an individual in which he or she notes that they were asleep "*en mi aposento.*"

Arancel: A tariff or established fee, usually as it related to a fine, administrative fees, or costs of legal proceedings. Throughout the Spanish colonial period the government established the maximum fees an official was allowed to charge for a service. Typically, *arancel* is mentioned in a manner that suggests the rates were periodically reviewed to prevent overcharging by *alcaldes* or other government officials who depended on these fees in lieu of a salary. Some documents even carry a certification that the fees charged were in compliance with established rates. The term also refers to fees paid to priests for various religious services. In one set of documents concerning this later usage, Mateo Garcia of Santa Fe complained to Governor Facundo Melgares in 1819 that the *cura* of Santa Fe wanted eighteen and a half pesos to perform a marriage. Garcia felt the charge was not only excessive, but that the priest unfairly refused to accept the equivalent in produce from the land (*productos de la tierra*) in lieu of cash. The document provides an interesting look not only at this type of fee structure, but the nature of New Mexico's colonial economics. Occasionally such fees for government services are called *derechos prosesales*.

Asonada: A riot or violent resistance. In 1831 the term is used to describe an incident in which the *genizaros* (Hispanicized Indians) of Abiquiú were suspected of threatening an uprising in opposition to the actions of a local official. A slang form of the term is still used to describe an assault or when someone is on the receiving end of a fight, such as when someone says, "*se lo sonaron.*"

Auto: An official statement or order, usually issued to show or declare compliance with some official business. An *auto de sentencia*, for example, would be the official notification of the imposition of a sentence or court order to the defendant. These usually include an elaborate statement of the authority by which the statement was issued.

Bartolina: A small cell or box used for detention or punishment of a prisoner. This may have been simply a small, windowless room, but the impression one gets from the few references to the use of this device at the jail in Santa Fe causes one to imagine "the box" made infamous by Paul Newman in the motion picture *Cool Hand Luke*.

Cambalache: A trade, usually by bartering, possibly derived from *cambio*, or *cambiar*. The term is still used in northern New Mexico to describe certain types of informal transactions, or trades. A 1797 document in which Manuel Trujillo was charged with stealing and bartering several horses (*robado y cambalachado*) uses it in this context.

Canje: In diplomatic terms, this is a formal exchange, such as when Spanish officials exchanged horses for several soldiers who had been taken prisoner by the Apache in 1779. The term is used differently from *rescate*, which is used throughout the colonial period to describe the formal "trade fairs" held with various Indian tribes along the New Mexican frontier. *Rescate* derives from the "rescues" or "ransom" of captives at these occasions. Many Spanish Archives documents refer to these events and the attempts by officials to regulate them. The difference between a *canje* and a *rescate* is explained in a 1778 document in which the Viceroy Theodore de Croix proposed to integrate official exchanges of prisoners, or *canjes*, at such times as when the customary *rescates* are held.

Careo: A face-to-face encounter or questioning of contending parties by an official investigating a crime or civil suit. This fascinating element of the Spanish judicial system was invoked when there was conflicting or inconsistent testimony. The parties who provided the conflicting testimony were brought together and the statements they had given read in front of the other person. The individuals were then asked to certify their testimony and given an opportunity to add to it or delete something they had said. When confronted in this procedure, defendants sometimes confessed, or the plaintiff in a civil case used this occasion to drop the charges.

Codisia: A desire for riches or vehement attempts to acquire the good things in life. It also means an impatience or anxiety to do something. This is not necessarily a bad or evil characteristic, but was viewed as an undesirable trait. In 1726, for example, the term is used to describe Spanish *vecinos'* greed in dealing unfairly with Indians at *rescates*.

Comisión: Often written as *comición*. Refers to the formal appointment or commission issued to an individual to perform a specific or limited task. Spanish governors, for example, often appointed a *jues comisionado* to hear a criminal case or conduct an investigation on their behalf. The degree of this commission varied. Some were commissions to investigate and prepare a case for review and sentencing by the governor. In some, however, the governor authorized the commissioner to actually decide a case and impose a sentence. In 1820, for example, Governor Facundo Melgares assigned José Antonio Chávez to handle a civil case for debt, *con comisión bastante*, or with full authority.

Denuncio: Typically, an accusation or denunciation by a complainant against a defendant. The term also refers to the formal notice of the charges being made against an individual.

Destierro: Exile; quite literally a sending away from your land or place of residence. Exile was a common form of punishment in both criminal and civil cases in Spanish colonial New Mexico. Exile was apparently permanent, but a few cases do specify a term. Santa Cruz de La Cañada, Bernalillo, Belen, and El Paso were among the places individuals were sent within New Mexico, but a few were also exiled to Chihuahua or Sonora.

Diligencias: Often written as *deligencias*, these are sworn testimony or statements in a civil or criminal case or other official proceeding. These statements were normally done under oath and in response to questions posed by an *alcalde* or other official. These are usually not verbatim but written in the second person by the official conducting the investigation. These statements are normally certified in the presence of witnesses. The most common use of the word is also applied to the large body of *diligencias matrimoniales*, or marriage investigations conducted by the Catholic Church during the Spanish, Mexican, and early Territorial periods.

Doncella: An unmarried female; a maiden or virgin. It usually refers to a young girl as when a fourteen-year-old used the word to describe herself when asked to state her name and status. It was also used in a 1684 rape case in which the presiding judge commented that it was a serious crime to "*desfloriar una doncella peqeña y mas contra su voluntad*" (deflower a young maiden, especially against her will). It may also refer to a servant in domestic service, particularly in service to the woman of the house.

Echisero: Refers to the casting of spells or bewitching. More specifically, the term refers to the person who makes or casts such spells. *Enechisado* is used in 1725 to identify a person upon whom a spell was cast. The term is not necessarily synonymous with witch, or *brujo*. One 1732 document refers to a stone that supposedly had the ability to help identify *echiseros*.

Embargo: A lien placed on the property or assets of an individual or corporate entity. These were usually done by order of a judicial officer to preserve the impounded property from being dissipated or lost pending the outcome of a case. The historical value of these liens comes from the detailed inventory and assessment of the property that provides us valuable information on the material culture of the time. After the property was embargoed and inventoried, it was usually placed under the guardianship or care of a *depositario de efectos* (guardian of the property). A *depositario*, however, sometimes referred to a person or household in which a minor or Indian servant was placed for safekeeping pending disposition of a case.

Embijes: Refers to the practice of painting of faces and /or bodies by Indian tribes, particularly in the context of preparing for battle or celebrating a victory. In 1714, Spanish officials debated the rights of Pueblos to do this and whether efforts of the Spanish to force the Pueblos to stop the practice may have infringed on their rights to perform certain ancient practices. In contemporary usage, someone who is constantly getting into trouble is sometimes said to be getting into or creating *embijes*.

Forastero: Technically, a person who is not a resident of the place he is currently located; an outsider. Some uses seem to indicate that the person may be a foreigner or individual without a permanent home, but not actually a vagabond. In the early eighteenth century, Governor Francisco Cuervo y Valdes noted that *forasteros* participated in the *rescates* held at Taos and Pecos, where they illegally traded horses to the Indians. The impression one gets is that the term may be the Spanish equivalent to "mountain man."

Fulano: Used in place of a name when the proper name is unknown or the writer chooses to ignore the given name of a person. Typically used as part of the phrase "*fulano de tal*." It can also be used as an insult, such as in an 1831 judicial proceeding against the *genizaros* of Abiquiú when an official referred to them as *fulanos de tal*, or "those so and so's."

Gale: Technically, a salary or wage. Probably a form of *jalar*, which means to work toward something or a goal, although it also refers to pulling or tugging on something. The term is not used very often in the Spanish archives but in one 1747 document, it is used to suggest that *alcaldes* cannot hold other jobs that pay a salary. Contemporary usage is slang for job or work.

Gandules: Derived from *gandul*, an individual in the military or militia of the Moors in Africa or Granada. An old definition refers to a vagabond, but the term is applied in the Americas specifically to wandering Indians who did not work the land and survived by hunting or fishing. The term was later applied in Mexico to the warriors of these tribes and is used as such in New Mexico throughout the Spanish and Mexican periods.

Grillos: Shackles or irons, as in *un par de grillos*. The hardware consisted of two shackles attached by a short chain. They seem to have been normally used to bind the ankles, but occasionally, documents specify that especially combative prisoners or those prone to escape were fettered with two pair, implying that they were to be used to tie the arms and legs. A smaller version, probably used only for the wrists are sometimes referred to as *grilletes*. An 1805 inventory of the property found in the Santa Fe *presidio* shows they had four pairs of *grillos* and one *grillete*.

Hijuela: In contemporary use, this usually refers to a property deed associated with a grant of land from the Spanish or

Mexican government. Historically, however, it is used to refer to a wide variety of assets or property. In 1818, for example, José Felipe Ortiz was charged and brought to trial for abusing his wife, Josefa Garcia, and wasting or mismanaging the assets (*su hijuela*) she had brought into the marriage, probably as a dowry.

Jusgado (also *juzgado*): The courtroom or place where judicial proceedings take place. The term is not used to indicate a jail, although the anglicized term "huzgow" usually implies a jail. A typical context in which judicial officials used the term was when they summoned someone to appear before them, such as *lo hice comparecer en este mi jusgado*.

Mohatrero: Probably a form of *mojigater(-ía)*, a word not found in most Spanish dictionaries. The word describes persons who interfere in business dealings, make trouble, cheat, or take unfair advantage of someone. This usage is from a July 2, 1790 viceregal *bando* (order) that regulated trade with the Pueblos. The order prohibited *mohatreros* from participating in this trade because they apparently conspired to purchase valuable commodities at a low price and resell them at a great profit.

Morada: Used in modern times to describe the chapel or meeting place of the *hermanos* (*penitents*), but historically used to describe a home or dwelling. References in numerous documents do not use the word in the context of a religious structure. Typical usage consists of the phrases "*mi casa morada*" and "*la morada de . . .*" A form of the word shows up in documents that describe the house where an individual lived as "*era donde moraba.*"

Moso: A servant or employee. References to these are often (but not always) in the context of a resident servant who lives in the household or otherwise belongs to the *amo*, or master of the house. Individuals typically identify themselves or are described as "*moso de . . .*" such-and-such a person or family. Many references to *mosos* relate to debts owed by the *moso* to his or her *amo*. It is possible that many of these individuals were in situations of debt servitude or peonage.

Olgasanería: Actually *holgazanería*, a form of *holgazán*; used to describe a person who is a vagabond, indolent, lazy, or has an aversion to work. In 1841, a vagabond and his family were tried and sentenced to Real del Oro, where he was to be put to work by local officials. The documents note the individual's life of *olgasanería*.

Pergamino: Technically parchment, but a 1785 document in the Spanish Archives uses the term to describe tanned, stretched beef hides of exceptional quality. These were apparently used for many purposes, including paintings and covers for books. In 1810 and 1814, Governor José Manrique noted students were using *pergamino* for their schoolwork because of an acute paper shortage.

Picota: A pillory. A vertical pole or stake to which a person could be tied. This pole was usually located on the plaza or other public place where individuals who had been sentenced to suffer a number of lashes could be tied. In 1761, Juan de la Cruz Valdez was sentenced to suffer fifty lashes *en una picota* after being found guilty of stealing a horse from an allied Ute tribe. In 1768 Governor Pedro Fermín Mendinueta specified a similar punishment of twenty-five lashes for persons of mixed blood (*de color quebrado*) caught stealing produce from the cultivated fields around Santa Fe. White persons convicted of this crime escaped the lashes, but were to be publicly humiliated by having them tied to the *picota* with the stolen produce draped around their neck.

Recua: A pack train, usually consisting of mules, but may have included horses or burros. It can also refer to any series of objects strung out in rows. The usage of *recua* differs from *cordón*, which was used to describe the scheduled commercial caravan that left New Mexico for Chihuahua and other points in Mexico. Archival documents contain many references to the schedule and regulation of the *cordon*, but seldom use the term *caravana* to describe it.

Rencidente: A form of the word *rencilla*; to be inclined to make trouble or to be troublesome or incorrigible. It may also be used to describe what we would today call a "habitual criminal." In 1841, for example, the *rencidente ladrón*, Pedro Mondragon, was exiled from New Mexico because he had been implicated in a series of thefts over a period of several years.

Reo: A person accused or suspected of a crime. Often used in the context of *reo en este causo* (suspect in this case), preceded by the name of the person. The term is also used to mean someone who was in custody or jail and is often synonymous for prisoner.

Rialengo: Probably *realengo*, used to describe vacant royal land or land that had been previously granted and abandoned. In 1768, the term was used in an application for a land grant at Ojo Caliente to describe a site that had been abandoned and declared "*por rialengo*." In Mexico, *relingo* refers to something that is tattered, ruined, abandoned, or in a wretched condition.

Riña: A quarrel or scuffle, usually involving several persons. The term was used in a case regarding a fight at San Jose de Las Huertas in 1811.

Sementeras, also *sementerías*: Planted and/or cultivated agricultural fields. A 1733 suit over an *acequia* used the word to describe the land irrigated by the ditch in question. Differs in use to *sembrados*, which also refers to planted fields, but seems to denote a smaller plot of land, such as a garden. Use of *sembardos* may indicate a planted field before it has begun to sprout or grow. *Labor* or *labores* are often used synonymously and a very similar word is used for cemetery.

Sepo (also *cepo* or *zepo*): Stocks used for punishment. No descriptions of these devices have been located in the archives, but they were probably similar to the wooden stocks which often illustrate the punishments used by our Puritan forefathers. In New Mexico, the use of stocks seems to have been more for preventing escape from confinement than for punishment. It is also not certain they were actually attached to a vertical pole. This type of device seems to have been more often used for the legs than for the arms and head, although on several occasions, sentences specified that prisoners were to be placed *de cabeza en el sepo* (with his head in the stocks). Despite their use, prisoners still managed to escape from New Mexico's notoriously inadequate jails. In 1767, for example, a prisoner escaped from the jail in Santa Fe after managing to remove his feet from the *sepo en que durmía* (the stocks in which he slept). An 1805 inventory shows the Santa Fe *presidio* had four *cepos de madera* (on stocks of wood). Another type of confinement was the *corma*, where the persons' feet were bound to a beam or board with rope or rawhide because *grillos* were not available. The term *bien cormado* is sometimes found in documents when officials are advised that a prisoner needs to be well secured, especially when he was being transported.

Index